20th CENTURY AMERICAN HISTORY FOR TEENS

20TH CENTURY AMERICAN HISTORY

★ FOR TEENS ★

Understanding the Movements, Policies, and Events that Changed Our World

Carrie Cagle

ROCKRIDGE
PRESS

Series Designer: Erin Yeung
Interior and Cover Designer: Karmen Lizzul
Art Producer: Sara Feinstein
Editor: Barbara J. Isenberg
Production Editor: Jenna Dutton
Production Manager: Martin Worthington

Photography used under license from Alamy, p. 3, 10, 23, 35, 42, 59, 62, 71, 73, 80, 92, 100, 102, 107, 114, 117, 124, 132, 135, Detroit Publishing Company, Prints and Photographs Division, Library of Congress, LC-USZC4-1584, p. 7; Library of Congress, Prints & Photographs Division, Farm Security Administration/Office of War Information Black-and-White Negatives, LC-USF33-T01-001128-M1, p. 19; Prints and Photographs Division, Library of Congress, LC-DIG-ppmsc-03521, p. 29; Prints and Photographs Division, Library of Congress, LC-USZ62-111201, p. 46; Prints and Photographs Division, Library of Congress, LC-DIG-ppmsca-19004, p. 56.

ISBN: Print 978-1-64876-223-9 | eBook 978-1-64876-224-6
R0

CONTENTS

INTRODUCTION x

CHAPTER 1:
INTO THE 20th CENTURY 1

Industrialization and the New Economy 2

Reconstruction and the Jim Crow Era 4

The "New" Immigration? 7

A Progressive Era 9

A Question of Isolation or Imperialism 12

Dawn of a New Century 14

CHAPTER 2:
PROGRESS AND THE END OF ISOLATION 17

Life in the 1900s 18

The Labor Movement 20

The Women's Suffrage Movement 22

The Great Migration 24

An Attempt at Neutrality 26

The United States Goes to War 28

CHAPTER 3:

PROSPERITY, DECLINE, AND WAR 33

1920s Culture: A Study in Contradictions 34

Politics and Economy in the 1920s:
A Return to Normalcy? 37

The Great Depression Descends, 1929–1933 39

The New Deal Begins to Lift the
Depression, 1933–1939 41

Attention Shifts Abroad 44

World War II 45

CHAPTER 4:

PEACE AND PROXY WARS 51

When They Came Home 52

A Time to Rebuild 55

The Marshall Plan and the Truman Doctrine 57

The Cold War, NATO, and the Warsaw Pact 60

Cold War Hotspots: Korea, Iran,
Vietnam, and Cuba 63

The Space Race 66

CHAPTER 5:
THE "GOLDEN" 1950s 69

The Golden Age of Capitalism 70

Babies in the 'Burbs 72

TVs and Tunes 76

The Civil Rights Movement 77

The Red Scare of the 1950s 81

Counterculture Movements:
   The Beats and Hippies 84

CHAPTER 6:
THE "RADICAL" 1960s 87

John F. Kennedy and the "New Frontier" 88

Lyndon B. Johnson and the "Great Society" 90

The Vietnam War 91

The Civil Rights Movement Continues 95

Black Power 98

The Stonewall Rebellion and the LGBTQ
   Rights Movement 101

CHAPTER 7:
ROOTS OF MODERN CONSERVATISM 105

Women's Liberation Movement 106

End of the Vietnam War: Peace
   but Not Honor 109

Nixon's Domestic Policies 111

A New Right 115

America in the Middle East 116

Reagan's Domestic Policies 118

CHAPTER 8:

CHANGE AT HOME AND ABROAD 123

The First Personal Computer 124

The Advent of the Internet 125

The Persian Gulf War 127

The End of the Cold War 129

The LA Riots 131

Gun Control 133

LEGACY 138

RESOURCES 141

SELECTED REFERENCES 144

INDEX 151

INTRODUCTION

Most people who have been traditionally educated have studied history in school. It's probably fair to say that if asked whether they liked history, more than half of those people (and maybe even something like two-thirds) would say "no." Unfortunately, history as it is taught can be pretty dull and is oftentimes composed of a stupefying list of dates, names, and vocabulary words that students memorize and quickly forget.

Yet it's likely that most people have at some point found some historically based form of media—maybe a movie, TV show, or video game—interesting. What makes historical entertainment so ... well ... entertaining? As a student of both history and psychology, I'd say that it's probably the focus on individuals as human beings, rather than as kings, generals, philosophers, founders of religions, and other typical history-making types that does the trick. Regardless of when historical characters lived, they were still *individuals*. It's just so cool to experience the stories of historical people who wore corsets, wielded swords, read hieroglyphics by candlelight, or worshipped Thor and Odin, yet still had the same kinds of feelings, dilemmas, and successes that we 21st-century people experience.

The lesson we can learn from historically based media is that *the way that history is presented matters*. Academic history can be nearly as interesting if we focus on how global events affected individuals' lives. Consider this quote from Aparna Basu, a historian from the University of Delhi: "History is no longer just a chronicle of kings and statesmen, of people who wielded power, but of ordinary women and men engaged in manifold tasks."

If you've had some bad experiences with history, you're not alone. I'd like to try to change that for you. I am a little biased, being a history teacher and all, but hear me out. I was bored to death by history in high school. Then I went to college and was forced to take Survey of Early American History for my liberal arts degree plan. I had a fantastic professor who yelled, cursed, waved his arms, jumped up on chairs, and ran around the room. This guy was so excited about history! He shared so much interesting stuff I never learned in high school. I decided to become a history teacher to make history less boring for high school students. So, a little propaganda here: For the sake of a poor, old high school teacher, please give history another chance.

A great reason to study history is to learn from our predecessors' successes and mistakes. You've probably heard some version of the Spanish philosopher George Santayana's saying, "Those who cannot remember the past are condemned to repeat it." Even if you don't plan to become a career politician, as a well-educated member of a democratic republic, being informed about the past can help you to think critically about the decisions you'll need to make as a voter. The purpose of this book is to help you do exactly that. The events of the 20th century brought us to where we are today, and developing a better understanding of those issues will make you a better citizen.

By now, you're probably raring to go with some history, right? However, there's one more thing to keep in mind: History is always told from a point of view. No author or teacher, no matter how determined to remain neutral, is completely unbiased. Even a historian who seems to be presenting plain old facts is still putting a spin on things simply by choosing which facts to present or emphasize and which facts to leave out. That is why it's important to use multiple sources of information when studying historical topics, in which you will hopefully find that similar information shows up. The moral of the story is to always consider history with a critical eye or ear, then come up with your own interpretation of events.

CHAPTER 1

INTO THE 20th CENTURY

It may be difficult to imagine, but the United States wasn't always one of the most powerful countries in the world. During the 20th century, certain events allowed the country to become dominant on the world stage. First, let's to look at what was going on in the late 19th century (the 1800s) for some context.

Industrialization and the New Economy

The time period between about 1865, when the Civil War ended, and 1900 is usually called the "Gilded Age." It really is a very fitting metaphor for the time period. A gilded object is made out of cheap metal and is then coated with a thin layer of gold. At a quick glance, a gold-coated item may look beautiful and shiny. Yet closer inspection may reveal its poor quality.

In much the same way, some aspects of the second half of the 19th century seem sparkly and attractive. For example, inventors created amazing new technologies, millionaires lived in gorgeous mansions, and fabulous World's Fair exhibitions displayed wonders of all sorts. On the flip side, factory workers lived in crowded slums, corrupt politicians ran amok, and business tycoons found ways to cheat people out of their money.

Both the sparkly and the corroded parts of the Gilded Age were due, in one way or another, to rapid industrialization. Americans went from producing items individually using human or animal labor to mass-producing items using machinery fueled by artificial power sources like steam or electricity. Before industrialization, most people lived on farms and grew, hand-made, or bartered with others for almost everything they needed. Industrialization moved much of working life from farms to factories, leading to the growth of cities (called urbanization).

Just after the Civil War, the United States started to become an economic powerhouse due to rapid industrialization. By 1900, the country was producing more steel—a key indicator of industrialization—than Great Britain and Germany combined.

A WORKER POSES NEXT TO A HORIZONTAL CORLISS STEAM ENGINE

What happened to cause all of this? While the southern states had seceded during the Civil War, the northern and western states, which came to be called the Union, just kept on holding Congress without them anyway. Technically, the decisions of Congress still applied to the southern states, because the Union never recognized the southern states' secession as legal. However, the southern Confederate states did not consider themselves part of the Union anymore, so they did not recognize the decisions Congress made. When the former Confederate states returned to the Union after the Civil War in a state of disgrace, they had to abide by the legislation that Congress had passed during their absence, even though their legislators had not gotten a say in those matters.

Because their economies were largely agricultural, the southern states tended not to vote for legislation encouraging industrialization. With the Confederate states gone, it was easier to move those laws along. This resulted in the Pacific Railway Act, which led to the development of the transcontinental railroad. Railroads' use of steel, iron, cloth for seats, and processed lumber for railroad ties created demand for factories and workers. Cities had large populations, due to increased immigration, so there were many people to fill those jobs. Additionally, the country had plenty of oil, coal, and iron to use as raw materials.

Corruption was rampant. In general, the government supported businesses, often looking the other way when shady deals helped business owners earn big bucks. Wealthy "robber barons," or businessmen who built their wealth through unfair, ruthless practices, created monopolies to control entire lines of production, from sourcing materials to final sale on the open market. Among the significant robber barons of that period were J. P. Morgan, Andrew Carnegie, and John D. Rockefeller. When governments tried to implement anti-monopoly laws, business owners found sneaky ways around those laws with trusts, or agreements between several businesses to join forces to control an entire sector or industry.

To make things worse, business and politics frequently got tangled up together. For instance, Union Pacific Railroad stockholders created a company called Crédit Mobilier and then sold or gave stocks to several congressmen and even the vice president. Those congressmen would then pass laws benefitting the railroads and look the other way when the company did something unethical or illegal. This was just one example of the kind of corruption that was common in the Gilded Age and that directly led to the Progressive Era.

Reconstruction and the Jim Crow Era

Reconstruction—that sounds nice, doesn't it? Maybe like someone accidentally knocked down your tower of blocks, but now you are going to work in harmony to build a new, better tower? Sometimes things are poorly named—like Reconstruction. This is the term for the years from 1865 to 1877, when the country was recovering from the Civil War.

The "Civil War amendments" are the Thirteenth, Fourteenth, and Fifteenth Amendments. The Thirteenth Amendment freed enslaved people. The Fourteenth Amendment made former enslaved people citizens and gave citizens equal protection under the law. The Fifteenth Amendment gave formerly enslaved men the right to vote.

But white Southerners who had treated Black people as inferior for their entire lives didn't simply wake up one day ready to embrace them as equals. During Presidential Reconstruction (1865–1867), President Andrew Johnson was strongly opposed to protecting the new federally guaranteed rights for Black Americans, and he didn't enforce the Civil War amendments. Southerners were allowed to create "Black codes," or sets of laws that treated Black Americans in much the same way they had been treated while enslaved. They also returned former Confederate leaders to power.

The second part of Reconstruction, Congressional Reconstruction (1867–1877), was much stricter. Radical Republicans in Congress, who were anti-slavery, had such a large majority that even if President Johnson vetoed their laws, they could override his vetoes. These Radical Republicans, who wanted to punish the South harshly, were essentially in control. They divided the South into five zones and used the military to enforce the law, including the three new amendments. Now Black Americans could vote and even hold political office.

Many white Southerners rebelled against these changes. Some responded with race riots and by forming the Ku Klux Klan and other such American hate groups. The contested presidential election of 1876 officially ended Reconstruction: Democrats and Republicans made a political deal, called the Compromise of 1877, to determine the winner of the election (Rutherford B. Hayes) in exchange for the removal of federal troops from the South.

Without troops there to enforce the new amendments, Southern Democrats subjected Black people to violence and discrimination once again. Southern lawmakers did this with Jim Crow laws, which violated Black people's civil rights. The laws also established the system of segregation, in which Black and white people used separate public facilities, such as water fountains, bus seats, restaurant sections, and schools. Segregation meant consistently inferior facilities and limited opportunities in every aspect of life for Black citizens. The beginnings of Jim Crow in the 19th century would influence and shape the 20th, leading to the civil rights movement in the 1940s through 1960s, as well as changing criminal justice and incarceration laws in the 1980s and 1990s.

FOCUS POINT: PLESSY V. FERGUSON

Homer Plessy, who was one-eighth African American and therefore legally a Black person according to Louisiana law, attempted to challenge a law requiring segregated seating on trains. In 1896, the Supreme Court ruled that the law was constitutional because separating the races did not keep them from having equal protection under the law as long as the facilities provided were equal. This decision upheld segregation, essentially declaring it to be constitutional, until 1954, when it was reversed by the *Brown v. Board of Education* decision.

The "New" Immigration?

Immigrants, another group that often experienced poverty and discrimination, greatly increased in numbers in the second half of the 19th century. We've all heard some version of a quote claiming that *everyone* in the United States is descended from an immigrant. That's because it's true. The most widely accepted theory is that the first people in the Americas migrated across a land bridge from modern-day Siberia about 20,000 years ago. These migrants are believed to be the ancestors of America's Indigenous peoples.

Even the Statue of Liberty was an immigrant, because she was a gift from France. The inscription on her base reads, "Give me your tired, your poor, your huddled masses yearning to breathe free ... " That inscription may sound welcoming, but we have to remember the theme of the Gilded Age: It looks great with a cursory, or quick, glance, but upon close examination, the truth is disappointing.

MULBERRY STREET IN NEW YORK CITY, AROUND 1900

Immigration itself was not new; what was new was the demographic makeup of the immigrants. Demographic makeup refers to population characteristics like religion, nationality, literacy levels, family size, and other such things. Before about 1870, most immigrants to the United States were from northern or western Europe—countries like England, France, Germany, Norway, and Sweden. Many of these immigrants were literate Protestants. (Protestantism is one of the major branches of Christianity, along with Catholicism and Orthodoxy.)

However, after 1870, different groups of immigrants began to arrive from central, eastern, and southern Europe. The cultures of these newcomers were different from those of their predecessors. Their religions included Judaism, Orthodox Christianity, and Catholicism. Some were associated with radical political ideas like socialism or anarchism. Due to their differences from previous groups of immigrants, they faced a lot of negative sentiment from "native-born" Americans (not to be confused with Indigenous peoples, those who are considered to be the original inhabitants of the Americas). This anti-immigrant attitude is known as nativism. Nativism was not a new phenomenon; Catholic Irish immigrants had been treated poorly for quite some time. Yet negative attitudes toward immigrants increased during the second half of the 19th century.

Many of these new immigrants came to the United States to escape religious persecution or political unrest at home. Most were very poor and were attracted by the availability of factory work in eastern US cities. They could live in immigrant enclaves, such as Little Italy in Chicago, where they could enjoy their compatriots' company and continue practicing some of their native customs. However, these communities were often overlooked by public officials who enforced building codes and sanitary conditions. As a result, factory-working immigrant families often lived in overcrowded tenements. These were poorly ventilated, multistory buildings, and it was not uncommon for 12 or more people to live together in a one-room apartment. In the west, Chinese immigrants began coming to the Pacific coast in large numbers in the late 1840s, attracted first by the California gold rush and later by the availability of railroad work. They too suffered from unequal pay and overcrowded living conditions.

In 1873, an economic downturn began, lasting for about 20 years. Native-born Americans began to complain about immigrants, especially Chinese immigrants, taking jobs away from them.

It was the Chinese who became the subject of America's first anti-immigration law. This was called the Chinese Exclusion Act, which did just that, excluding Chinese individuals from the country for about 80 years, beginning in 1882. While other immigrant groups would not be officially limited until after the turn of the century, this was a sort of harbinger, or indicator, of what was to come.

A Progressive Era

To sum up, the Gilded Age left America with some cool new inventions, a globally dominant economy, and a whole heap of problems. Industrialization had given people easy access to fairly inexpensive manufactured goods. However, this cheap manufacturing process required factories, in which owners were free to treat their employees as they pleased. No legislation to protect workers' health and well-being existed yet. Employees could be forced to work incredibly long shifts (often without a break), did not have to be paid a minimum wage, and were usually not given any kind of safety gear or health care. Child labor was very common. Small children were especially useful in clothing factories, where they could crawl under machines and fetch fallen objects, and in mines, where they could squeeze into tight spaces.

Additionally, the realization of a workable lightbulb and electric power grid made working conditions worse. Now factories could operate after dark and workers could be forced to put in even longer hours.

Industrialization spurred urbanization, which created additional problems. Skyscrapers were made possible by the invention of the elevator and a new process for making steel. This allowed cities to grow in capacity. Both migrants and immigrants flocked to cities like New York, Chicago, and Philadelphia in search of jobs. The poorer residents lived in terrible, crowded conditions.

Jacob Riis, a police reporter, entered dark tenements to document the reality of life in a New York slum, using the newly invented technology of flash photography. His photographs were first published in newspapers, then later in a book called *How the Other Half Lives*. He believed that by exposing the problems of the cities, he could generate interest in reform. This form of journalism—called muckraking, as if the reporters were raking or stirring up muck—kicked off the Progressive Era.

LODGERS IN A CROWDED BAYARD STREET TENEMENT IN NEW YORK CITY, LATE 19TH OR EARLY 20TH CENTURY

Riis and other journalists began to expose all kinds of issues of the Gilded Age society. They shone light on things like child labor (Lewis Hine), the meatpacking industry (Upton Sinclair), the corporate world (Ida Tarbell), political corruption (Lincoln Steffens), racism (Ida B. Wells and W. E. B. Du Bois), and women's rights (Margaret Sanger).

The muckrakers' exposés were a feature of the Progressive Era, the period from around 1890 until 1920. Progressive thinkers and politicians believed they could apply reason and scientific findings to improve society and solve the problems created by the Gilded Age. The strides toward greater social justice these reformers made served as the foundation for later movements.

UP FOR DEBATE: SOCIAL DARWINISM

While muckrakers and progressive reformers felt that helping the urban poor was necessary, others believed that the lower classes should essentially be ignored. These Social Darwinists based their arguments on Charles Darwin's theory of evolution. Darwin argued that in the biological world, it was natural for some species to survive and for others to die off due to their inability to adapt to their environments. Social Darwinists applied this idea to different groups of human beings, saying some groups of people would dominate other groups and that was just part of nature. This argument was used to justify mistreatment of the poor and white imperialism. Darwin himself was absolutely appalled by Social Darwinism and refused to have anything to do with it.

A Question of Isolation or Imperialism

Since the Mexican-American War ended in 1848, the United States had been pretty isolationist. But in 1890, America reached a turning point. The federal government declared the western frontier closed, meaning that there would be no more western continental expansion. Expansionism had long been part of American culture, though, and Americans were still eager to look outside the United States' borders for new places to expand, or become imperialist. Imperialism involves the building of an empire, and to build an empire one country has to take over other countries and either absorb them or turn them into colonies. There were a lot of arguments to support this idea: The country could use more markets for its goods; Americans could spread their culture and religion to other nations, most of which Americans felt were uncivilized; and most important, overseas expansion would place the United States on a tier of highly developed countries that had also expanded overseas.

The problem was that the United States was late to the party, and there was very little unclaimed land left. However, in 1895, José Martí led Cuba in a rebellion against Spain (its colonial ruler). Cuba is only 90 miles southeast of Florida, and a lot of wealthy Americans had money invested in sugar plantations there, so the United States was very interested in this rebellion. The Spanish sent a brutal general to squelch the rebellion. This general moved about 300,000 Cubans into restrictive camps.

Shocking newspaper coverage of the situation in Cuba, the interception of a Spanish letter criticizing President William McKinley, and the mysterious explosion of an American ship in a Cuban harbor led to the Spanish-American War in 1898. The United States won the war in less than four months,

and in the 1898 Treaty of Paris, Spain ceded the islands of
Cuba, Guam, and Puerto Rico to the United States. It also sold
the Philippines for $20 million. The Philippines was to be
annexed, or added on, to the United States, and the other three
islands essentially became protectorates, or territories dependent on a more powerful country.

The United States had now, in a sense, become a colonial power itself and was now doing almost exactly the
same thing that it had criticized the Spanish for doing in
Cuba. In response, a rebellion sprang up in the Philippines
against American occupation. After three years, the rebellion was squashed, and the United States established an
American-dominated government that kept the Philippines
under its control until after World War II.

MATTER OF CHOICE:
WAR WITH SPAIN

President McKinley didn't want to go to war with Spain.
He believed that Spain must not continue to put Cubans
into camps and tried his best to negotiate a diplomatic
solution with Spain. The problem was with public
opinion. Americans had been whipped into a frenzy
by yellow journalism, a type of sensationalist writing
that embellished the truth to sell newspapers. In defer-
ence to popular opinion, Congress declared war on
April 25, 1898.

Dawn of a New Century

With immigration increasing, business booming, and a growing presence on the world stage, the United States kicked off the last year of the 19th century with a presidential election, a rematch between William McKinley, the incumbent president, and William Jennings Bryan, who was considered to be an "anti-imperialist." McKinley's reelection was viewed as a thumbs-up to American imperialism. However, not everyone approved of McKinley. In 1901, he was assassinated. Upon McKinley's death, Vice President Theodore Roosevelt, who also promoted expansionist policies, became the next president.

Roosevelt believed that the federal government's role was to ensure the welfare of the people, and he used his executive (presidential) power freely to accomplish this. To preserve spaces for enjoying outdoor pursuits, he supported conservation of public parks. In fact, he established the forest system and national parks. As a progressive, he would not stand for political corruption.

As the 20th century rolled in, the United States was on the rise from a foreign relations standpoint. The efficiency of industrial production had strengthened the American economy and allowed the country to establish strong trade partnerships with other nations. Politically, the growth of the US Navy and the country's victory in the Spanish-American War made it a kind of junior world power.

Domestically, the United States still had many problems, including political corruption, poor working conditions, a lack of civil rights for people of color and women, nativism, and poverty. Yes, the progressive movement was working on those, but it had just begun.

CHAPTER 2

PROGRESS AND THE END OF ISOLATION

Remember when you were younger and preparing for a birthday? You'd think that you were going to wake up that day and be somehow *changed*—more mature, smarter, better looking, and definitely taller. Of course, that didn't happen. Similarly, just because a new century arrived didn't mean that society transformed. Instead, the movements that had begun at the end of the 19th century—progressive reform and America's growing influence in the world—continued to gradually change American society and politics.

Life in the 1900s

Many of us dream about being transported back in time, but rarely do we picture a historical romp back to 1901, and there's a reason for that: Life in the early 20th century was pretty tough and mostly about work. How Americans at the start of that century lived their lives depended largely on circumstances outside their control, such as where they were born and the color of their skin.

A Day in the Life of Clarence Farnsworth

Sixteen-year-old Clarence wakes up before dawn. He does about two hours of farm chores like milking cows, cleaning horses' stalls, and feeding chickens with his brothers and father before heading inside for breakfast.

His mother and 12-year-old sister, Edith, have been up since before dawn, too, making breakfast from scratch. They have fresh milk, coffee, eggs, ham, biscuits, and butter. The family eats well because even without a refrigerator, their animals give them access to fresh food.

After breakfast, Ma and Edith will spend most of their day cooking, preparing to cook, or cleaning up after cooking. Any spare time will be spent sewing clothes for the family, doing laundry by hand, or working in the garden. The family does not own any modern equipment like a washing machine, dishwasher, or sewing machine.

Clarence and Pa drive the horse-drawn wagon to collect rent from the sharecroppers, Black tenants who live on the Farnsworths' land. They can't afford to pay cash rent, so they give the Farnsworths a share of their crops instead. The Freeman family is short four bushels of cotton. Pa makes a funny sound in his throat and declares, "I'll add it to next year's numbers." Mr. Freeman looks ashamed; it seems like the system is set up so that the sharecroppers are always just a little bit short.

A NORTH CAROLINA SHARECROPPER, AROUND 1938

A Day in the Life of Alessandra Ricci

Thirteen-year-old Alessandra wakes up at 5:00 a.m. when one of her sisters kicks her in the stomach. All six of the kids sleep on one big bed in the corner that folds up into the wall during the day. They need the extra space, since they live in a one-room tenement apartment in New York City with her parents, grandmother Nonna, and uncle. She dresses quickly, washing with a bit of cloth and some water from a bucket that she brought up from the pump in the street last night. Then she bundles up in a shawl her mother bought at the second-hand store and goes downstairs to use the outhouse in the courtyard. It's a terrible place to live, but it's all Alessandra's family can afford, even now that she is working.

After breakfast, Alessandra goes to the shirtwaist factory, where she will sew stylish blouses for beautiful American ladies. On the way, she passes the high school, envying the students who get to learn all day because they don't have to work.

Upon reaching the factory, she rides the electric elevator to the ninth floor. It's so amazing to be carried up nine stories by a simple cable! The workroom is difficult to navigate due to the small buckets of water, boxes of fabric scraps, and closely spaced work tables, but she finally makes it to her machine at the far end.

She's just in time. She hears the click of the floor boss locking the doors from the outside just as she sits down. The girls are locked in all day to prevent them from stealing. They will also be searched before they leave at the end of their shift at 6:00 p.m.

Alessandra's friend Luca hands her a pamphlet. "Put it in your pocket for now," Luca whispers. "We can't let the bosses see. But we can join together and get the bosses to treat us better! It's called a union. There's one just for us—the International Ladies' Garment Workers' Union."

Alessandra pockets the pamphlet and vows to take it with her to her English class tomorrow night at the settlement house. Maybe one of the teachers will help her read it. She would certainly like to be treated better at work.

The Labor Movement

The women of the International Ladies' Garment Workers' Union weren't the only ones campaigning for better working conditions. In the late 19th and early 20th centuries, workers were treated as commodities—something that can be bought or sold—not human beings. With a seemingly endless stream of new immigrants entering the country every year, protections for these workers were few and far between. The government did not regulate things like working hours, minimum wage, the right to unionize, health care, and sick leave.

At the turn of the century, there were about 30,000 deaths and one million injuries per year in factories. The average male worker in 1900 worked six days a week, for a total of 60 to 65 hours per week. Male factory workers weren't paid enough to support their families on their own. So, while middle- and upper-class women rarely worked outside the home, almost all lower-class women did. Even children as young as three were sent to work in factories.

Samuel Gompers was one of the first and the loudest voices for labor rights in the United States. He formed the American Federation of Labor in 1886. Its goals included shortening the workday, ending child labor, improving standards of living for workers, and a guarantee of the right to collective bargaining. It and other labor organizations had organized strikes in the Gilded Age. But in every case, the federal government had intervened on the side of management, forcing the workers to continue working under abusive conditions.

During the Progressive Era, the outcomes of labor disputes began to change in favor of workers. In 1902, a strike by coal miners threatened to shut off the heat supply to several major American cities in the middle of winter. President Theodore Roosevelt got involved as a neutral arbitrator, or go-between, to help the mine-workers' union and management reach an agreement. This was a turning point in the federal government's attitude toward strikes.

In 1904, a group of prominent social welfare activists organized the National Child Labor Committee (NCLC). The group backed the Keating-Owen Act of 1916, which made child labor illegal using the Constitution's commerce clause: As the federal government has the right to regulate interstate commerce, or any business that crosses state lines, the act said the government could also determine *how* those businesses conducted their affairs. Unfortunately, the Supreme Court struck down the Keating-Owen Act in 1918 with the case of *Hammer v. Dagenhart*. It ruled that factory production itself was not commerce, and so was up to the states to regulate. Child labor would not be effectively controlled at the federal level again until nearly 20 years later with the Fair Labor Standards Act of 1938.

Despite all the progress being made at the legislative and court level, many disasters still struck, like the one at the New York Triangle Shirtwaist Factory in 1911. When a fire broke out on March 25, 1911, a huge array of fire hazards, including locked, inward-swinging exit doors, a fire escape that only went down to the sixth floor, tables that blocked exit routes, and a lack of fire hoses, resulted in the deaths of 146 of 500 workers. This fire led to the creation of the New York Factory Investigating Commission. The commission wrote 36 new safety bills, which were signed into law in New York and served as models for laws in other states.

Overall, the Progressive Era's labor movement was best at making Americans aware that reform was necessary and inspiring public sympathy for laborers. Tragic events like the Triangle Shirtwaist fire, the work of journalists like Lewis Hine, and the formation of large unions like the American Federation of Labor brought to light the need for change. However, by the end of the Progressive Era, the labor movement had only taken baby steps, leaving plenty of issues for future eras to address.

The Women's Suffrage Movement

Women had begun petitioning for expanded rights earlier in the century and continued to do so in this time period. In 1848, the first American women's rights convention had been held at Seneca Falls, New York. Women argued that they were more religious than or morally superior to men. As voters, they would then be less prone to use warfare and more likely to promote the welfare of society. They even argued that it was wrong for literate, educated white women to be denied the right to vote, while illiterate Black men were granted suffrage. Indeed, most early women's rights organizations fought for suffrage only for white women.

A WOMAN DEMONSTRATES FOR EQUAL RIGHTS FOR WOMEN, 1910S

Their arguments went against a long-standing cultural ideal called "separate spheres." This philosophy held that men belonged in the public sphere of work, politics, and business, while women belonged in the private sphere of the home. Women could have influence over politics by quietly suggesting things to their husbands at home. Then their husbands could decide whether their wives' opinions had any merit and let that influence their own votes if they thought so.

In 1890, several women's organizations combined to form the National American Woman Suffrage Association (NAWSA). This organization was created to focus on both women's suffrage and other women's issues, like temperance, charity work, and workplace equality. By the early 20th century, the suffragists' work was beginning to pay off. Western states began allowing women to vote in state elections.

At the national level, though, the so-called progressive presidents—Theodore Roosevelt, William Howard Taft, and Woodrow Wilson—did not support women's suffrage (though Roosevelt did support it later).

Then along came Alice Paul, a militant activist who formed a more radical organization, the National Women's Party (NWP). Her efforts included marching in the 1913 suffrage procession and later picketing the White House for 18 months.

More mainstream suffragists decided to cast their activism aside for the duration of World War I and instead became involved in war industry and relief efforts. Women served as nurses, telephone operators, ambulance drivers, factory workers, fundraisers, and leaders of food conservation efforts. Their efforts helped turn public opinion (including that of President Wilson) in favor of women's suffrage. In 1918, Wilson endorsed the Nineteenth Amendment, granting women the right to vote. The amendment was ratified in 1920.

The Great Migration

Much like the labor union members and suffrage activists, Black people who suffered discrimination in the South were also ready for change.

After the Civil War, there was a period of Reconstruction during which federal troops enforced the equal protection guaranteed by the Fourteenth Amendment. Unfortunately, once those troops left in 1877, white people just found ways to re-create many circumstances of the system of slavery under a different name—Jim Crow. The 1896 Supreme Court case *Plessy v. Ferguson* legally sanctioned segregation.

Many Black people worked as sharecroppers, which was almost as bad as being enslaved. Sharecroppers rented a bit of land and some tools from white landowners; then when the harvest came in, they paid their rent with an often larger-than-was-fair share of the crop. After they paid the landlord, their remaining share wasn't enough to live on, so they were always in debt to the landlord. States found ways around allowing Black people to vote, too—like imposing poll taxes they couldn't afford or literacy tests they couldn't pass. On top of that, Black people also faced social discrimination and violence.

Starting around 1915, waves of Southern Black people began to move to northern cities both in search of factory work and to escape segregation. About six million people moved over a period of 55 years. This urban demand for workers was created by the absences of male workers who had enlisted in World War I, and later because of restrictions on immigration.

Of course, there was still racism in the North, called de facto racism. That's racism by custom rather than by law. Black people were excluded from living in whole parts of cities and from union membership, leading to the creation of some vibrant Black-oriented neighborhoods in large cities, such as Harlem in New York.

This diaspora, or spreading out, of Black people from the rural South to the urban North and West also helped spread some cultural movements. Ragtime and jazz music flowed from New Orleans to cities like New York, St. Louis, and Kansas City. Artistic and cultural movements like the New Negro movement and the Harlem Renaissance also resulted from the Great Migration.

In the summer of 1918, a pandemic broke out that was caused by a new strain of flu virus that infected adults between 20 and 45 years old—a normally healthy population. Flu vaccines, antibiotics, mechanical ventilators, and other modern medical technology had yet to be invented, and World War I had caused shortages of physicians and medical supplies. Additionally, the movement of troops returning home from the war hastened the spread of the disease. As a result, the Spanish flu infected 28% of the world population and killed 10 times more Americans than World War I.

An Attempt at Neutrality

World War I, the event that signifies the end of the Progressive Era, affected all three of the groups we've been examining in this chapter in one way or another. It caused a great demand for war materials, which naturally would affect factory workers by forcing them to ramp up production. Women's involvement in the war effort changed public opinion in their favor and allowed them to finally win suffrage in 1920. Additionally, the availability of factory jobs in the North attracted Black people from the South, leading to the Great Migration. But how and why did the United States get involved in this war in the first place?

Since the Spanish-American War, the United States had pretty much stayed in its own hemisphere. Actually, Theodore

Roosevelt had even issued a statement, called the Roosevelt Corollary, urging European countries to restrict themselves to the Eastern Hemisphere. It promised that, in return, the United States would serve as a sort of policeman of the Western Hemisphere.

There were five causes of the war in Europe: militarism, an arms race, imperialism, nationalism, and entangling alliances. The first two were kind of related. Militarism is the glorification of the military and war, and an arms race is a situation in which countries begin to stockpile weapons, usually as a result of militarism.

Next were imperialism and nationalism, which are also related. Imperialism is the desire to acquire colonies. European countries had been competing over the acquisition of colonies for several centuries. Nationalism often occurs as a result of imperialism; it is the desire to live in a country ruled by people of one's own nationality. Several huge empires in Europe (like the Austro-Hungarian Empire and the Ottoman Empire) had overtaken many small nations, and those nations wanted to break free and rule themselves again.

All of this led to the fifth reason for the war: entangling alliances. The alliance system was complicated and secretive and shifted around frequently. Once the war started in 1914, the two warring sides were the Allies—Great Britain, France, and Russia—and the Central Powers—Germany, Austria-Hungary, Bulgaria, and eventually the Ottoman Empire.

In summary, a giant mess in Europe led to the declaration of war in Europe in August 1914. The United States had a long-standing tradition of diplomatic neutrality. Additionally, the US military didn't seem up to the task of dealing with a land war in Europe. However, the United States continued to trade with and loan money to both sides. Since Americans shared some cultural ties with the Allies, the United States lent more money and sold more goods to them. The Germans felt that violated the United States' declared neutrality, though, and their U-boats (submarines) started torpedoing American ships.

In 1915, a British passenger ship, the *Lusitania*, was sunk by German torpedoes, killing 123 American passengers. To many Americans, it seemed like the Germans were being ruthless and dishonorable.

The United States Goes to War

For the first two years, the war in Western Europe was essentially a stalemate. The Allies and the Central Powers were fairly evenly matched on the Western Front, where France and Germany engaged in trench warfare that led nowhere.

The German government realized it could gain an edge on the Western Front by cutting off American supplies being shipped to the Allies. Germany stepped up its torpedoing of American ships, making Americans even angrier with Germany.

Then came the final straw: the Zimmermann Telegram, sent from a German ambassador to a Mexican ambassador. It proposed that if Mexico would ally itself with Germany, then Germany would reward Mexico with California, New Mexico, Arizona, and Texas. Mexico politely declined, but the telegram was a huge diplomatic error. About a month after news of the telegram was leaked to the press, in April 1917, President Wilson asked Congress to declare war on Germany.

It was challenging for the United States to mobilize, or get things moving, for its involvement in the war at first. Companies that manufactured war goods had already sold many of their products to Allied buyers for the spring and summer. This made it difficult for the US government to get some necessary items. Also, the United States didn't keep a standing army, so it was necessary to enlist soldiers. The Selective Service Act of 1917 helped fill the ranks of the armed forces by requiring physically fit men between the ages of 21 and 30 to enlist.

A POSTER FROM THE UNITED STATES ARMY ENCOURAGING YOUNG MEN TO ENLIST IN THE MILITARY

To support the effort to "keep the world safe for democracy," the US government also created the Committee on Public Information. This was essentially a propaganda factory. This agency put out some very questionable posters and newspaper ads. It even issued a series of guidelines for newspapers to follow to ensure they remained appropriately patriotic.

The United States limited some of its citizens' civil liberties in the interest of wartime safety. The Espionage Act of 1917 made it illegal to give out information designed to help the country's enemies in a time of war. This legislation stemmed from fears about immigrants who might be tempted to send sensitive information to their home countries.

UP FOR DEBATE:
SCHENCK V. UNITED STATES

In 1918, two socialists, Charles Schenck and Elizabeth Baer, were passing out fliers encouraging people to peacefully resist the draft. They were prosecuted under the Sedition Act, which led to the Supreme Court case *Schenck v. United States*. The question was: Can the government deny people freedom of speech in certain situations? The court's decision was that the government *can* limit Americans' speech in times of "clear and present danger." A general fear of "undemocratic" thought systems, particularly communism, would continue into the 1920s, resulting in a Red Scare and several anti-immigration laws.

The Russian Revolution of 1917, in which the monarchist government was overthrown by communists, also contributed to an American suspicion of "radicals," like communists, socialists, and anarchists. Such radicalism was also associated with immigrants from Eastern and Central Europe. (This was similar to many people's suspicion of Middle Eastern and Muslim individuals that occurred after the 9/11 terrorist attacks.) As a result, the Sedition Act of 1918 criminalized any kind of unpatriotic speech or interference with the government's wartime activities.

MATTER OF CHOICE:
THE TREATY OF VERSAILLES

President Wilson was planning for a peace treaty even before World War I was over. He wrote a document called the Fourteen Points, which was meant to create "a peace without victory" by promoting the self-determination of nations (meaning that countries would get to choose their own forms of government), along with free trade, open agreements, and the creation of a League of Nations for settling disputes between countries. The other European leaders at the Paris Peace Conference held after the war focused on punishing Germany by severely limiting its military. They also imposed reparations on Germany, which required the country to pay to repair the damage caused during the war. The final Treaty of Versailles *did* include a League of Nations, but the United States did not sign the treaty because some members of Congress did not agree with it. As a result, the United States did not join the League of Nations. The weakness of the treaty and the failure of the League of Nations contributed directly to the rise of Nazi Germany and the arrival of World War II.

CHAPTER 3

PROSPERITY, DECLINE, AND WAR

Once the Great War (as World War I was called at the time) was over, Americans hoped to get back to normal in the 1920s, as many enjoyed a period of economic prosperity. Unfortunately, the stock market crashed in 1929, leading to 10 years of economic depression. While President Franklin D. Roosevelt's New Deal helped America partially recover, only the demand for munitions—military weapons, equipment, and ammunition—created by World War II fully brought the Depression to an end.

1920s Culture: A Study in Contradictions

In 1920, about 54 million Americans (more than half the US population) lived in cities. This was the first time in US history that more of the population lived in cities than in rural areas. There were simply more jobs available in cities. Due to the Great Migration, Black culture continued to flourish, leading to what some called the "Jazz Age" in the 1920s because of the popularity of jazz music.

In the 1920s, the availability of work for middle-class white women increased. Certain office jobs were beginning to be considered "women's jobs," so more middle-class women worked outside the home as secretaries, telephone operators, or receptionists. For white women of this social class, it was considered acceptable to work only before they were married. Meanwhile, poorer immigrant and Black women remained stuck with low-paying factory or domestic work, so they were often forced to continue working even after marriage to support their families.

New opportunities for work outside the home, along with other developments in society, changed the general idea of how white, middle- and upper-class women were supposed to behave. First, new technologies were making housework easier for women who could afford things like washing machines, vacuum cleaners, and electric mixers. Second, due to the work of Margaret Sanger and the Birth Control Clinical Research Bureau, doctors were now able to legally prescribe some early forms of birth control. As a result, women who could afford the doctors' fees could choose to have fewer children.

JOSEPHINE BAKER (ON THE RIGHT, HOLDING THE PEARLS), A PROMINENT SINGER AND DANCER, IN FRANCE IN 1906

Flappers were the most extreme symbol of women's increased freedom. A flapper was a rebellious young woman who cut her hair short, wore shorter skirts, smoked and drank in public, and went out with men without a chaperone. While expectations of women kept changing throughout the 20th century, flappers helped normalize behavior that today is part of everyday life for women in the United States.

Other types of social change occurred in the 1920s as well. One was the rise of consumer culture—the idea that spending money on certain products will help us achieve a lifestyle that will make us happy. This happened partially as a result of all the industrialization that occurred in the last part of the 19th century, which made factory products plentiful and less expensive.

All this change wasn't everyone's cup of tea. Prohibition, or the Eighteenth Amendment, went into effect in January 1920. It made the manufacture, sale, and transportation of alcohol illegal. Some of the proponents of Prohibition argued that making alcohol unavailable would decrease domestic crimes, while others adopted religious or moral arguments against alcohol.

But Prohibition just didn't work. Psychologically, banning something can make it more attractive to certain types of people. Others were addicted to alcohol and were willing to pay smugglers' high prices. Additionally, the federal government did not enforce Prohibition well. Some of the effects of Prohibition were the rise of organized crime (due to the Mafia's smuggling activities) and a loss of federal income from taxing legal alcohol. For these reasons, the Twenty-First Amendment repealed Prohibition in 1933.

UP FOR DEBATE: TEMPERANCE MOVEMENT

The temperance movement, which went back to the 19th century, had one goal: to prevent people from drinking alcohol. The reasons for promoting temperance varied. Some groups wanted to ensure that workers were more reliable, while others cited religious justifications. In the Progressive Era, groups like the Women's Christian Temperance Union saw it as a feminist issue, as husbands and fathers with alcohol addiction might become abusive, while nativists sometimes associated alcohol use with immigrant groups.

Politics and Economy in the 1920s: A Return to Normalcy?

The presidential campaign of Warren G. Harding was based on the slogan "a return to normalcy." Harding's stated desire to bring the country back to a more politically relaxed state after the twin traumas of World War I and the 1918 flu pandemic spread through the decade. Presidents Harding, Calvin Coolidge, and Herbert Hoover were all Republicans who supported isolationism and laissez-faire policies. "Laissez-faire" means "let it be" in French and refers to a lack of government interference in the economy. These presidents did very little to enforce the Progressive Era legislation designed to regulate businesses. As a result, some parts of the economy—like big corporations, banks, and the stock market—became extremely profitable.

Furthermore, businesses had a lot to work with, thanks to technology! Though it had been invented at the end of the 19th century, the automobile really took off in the 1920s. Henry Ford developed the assembly line, which allowed the less expensive mass production of cars. An increased demand for automobiles stimulated other industries needed for making cars, like glass, steel, and rubber. Of course, cars needed roads to drive on, so the road construction industry also flourished. People's increased mobility allowed them to live farther away from work as well, so suburbs sprang up, stimulating the housing construction industry.

However, in keeping with our 1920s theme of contradictions, some parts of the economy, such as the agricultural sector, were not doing so well. During World War I, warring European countries had needed to import more food than usual. American farmers had been happy to invest in new agricultural technology, so they could produce more crops to profitably sell to Europe.

After a few years of recovery from the war, European countries were able to grow their own food again and no longer needed the US imports. Unfortunately, many US farmers had bought farm machinery on credit and needed to pay those bills, so they kept growing huge crops, leading to overproduction. To understand why this was a problem, we need to understand the economic idea of supply and demand. Consider Halloween candy sales: Halloween candy goes on sale on November 1 because the store has too much of it and nobody wants Halloween candy anymore. Stores drop the price drastically to get rid of it quickly. In other words, when there is too much of something (the supply is high) and not many people want it (the demand is low), the price for that thing drops.

That's what happened with the farmers' crops in the 1920s: There were too many farm goods that no one wanted, so prices plummeted. While cheaper food might be good for consumers, it wasn't good for farmers, who weren't making enough money to pay their bills.

US loans to European countries, the increased use of credit buying, and stock market speculation were also problematic. Hoping to prevent another European war, the United States loaned money to Germany so that it could make reparations payments to France. Additionally, more and more Americans were buying on credit, but there were no regulations at the time to control how much credit banks and stockbrokers could extend, leading many people to get into more debt than they could pay back.

Credit buying even extended to the stock market, where investors could buy shares of corporations. They bought stocks "on margin," which meant that they would pay for only part of the stock, and stockbrokers would lend them the rest of the money. The idea was that the stock would quickly earn investors enough money to pay back their stockbrokers. This worked out as long as the price of stocks kept rising. Most thought that the stock market would keep expanding forever, but it didn't.

On October 29, 1929, these weaknesses in the economy that had existed throughout the 1920s—overproduction, credit buying, and stock market speculation—came together to cause the stock market to crash. That marked the beginning of the Great Depression. Lasting from 1929 to 1939, the Great Depression was the worst economic downturn in the 20th century.

The Great Depression Descends, 1929–1933

People lost confidence in the economy as a result of the 1929 stock market crash. They stopped making new investments and began spending less money, leading some businesses to lay off workers.

Many economists in the late 1920s believed that the depression was simply part of the business cycle. This is a sort of "what goes up must come down" theory. The idea is that economies go through normal fluctuations (ups and downs), so that after a period of prosperity or a "boom," an economy will naturally even itself out with a period of recession or even depression. Therefore, theoretically, when a recession or depression occurs, all that's necessary is to wait it out.

So instead of enacting programs to provide people with government relief, President Hoover spoke of "rugged individualism"—the idea that economic success was the product of individual hard work and sacrifice. According to this idea, the government was not responsible for helping those who were struggling. Instead, those individuals should figure out a way to solve their economic problems themselves.

The attempts that the Hoover administration did make to alleviate the economic pain caused by the stock market crash backfired. Hoover signed an extremely high tariff (a tax on imports) into law in 1930, figuring that making imports more expensive to buy would protect American manufacturing. Unfortunately, this just led to other countries passing tariffs on American goods in return, making US goods more expensive to buy abroad.

Additionally, in 1931, Hoover created the Reconstruction Finance Corporation to loan money to banks, railroads, and businesses. Unfortunately, the requirements to obtain the loans were very strict and the program didn't help many people.

Meanwhile, Americans' economic problems were worsening. The number of people without jobs climbed from around 3% in the summer of 1929 to near 25% by 1932. Economists consider a 5% unemployment rate to be normal, so clearly the economy was in dire straits. Marriage and birth rates declined. The suicide rate went up 40%. About 1.2 million Americans were homeless.

Many had lost their savings through no fault of their own. Knowing that banks were not regulated, people would withdraw all of their money from banks to ensure they had cash on hand. It was common to see long lines of people outside the banks waiting to withdraw their money. When the banks ran out of cash, they simply closed. Those who hadn't gotten their money out in time simply lost their savings. A total of about $140 billion simply disappeared between 1929 and 1933. This caused about 9,000 banks to fail.

For those who lived in the Great Plains (Colorado, Kansas, Nebraska, New Mexico, Oklahoma, and Texas), environmental issues added insult to injury. A severe drought began in 1930, and dust storms arrived in 1931. The lack of water made farming impossible and the dust storms made breathing difficult. Some of the residents of these so-called "Dust Bowl" states migrated to California in search of farm work, but California already had too many out-of-work farm laborers to begin with, so jobs were scarce.

Religious organizations and private charities provided some relief, such as soup kitchens and bread lines. But for the most part, Americans simply suffered. New slang terms came into use that demonstrated a general resentment toward the Hoover administration for not doing more to help. For example, a homeless camp made up of tents or shanties was called a "Hooverville."

The New Deal Begins to Lift the Depression, 1933–1939

Franklin D. Roosevelt (often referred to as "FDR" to differentiate him from his distant cousin, Theodore Roosevelt) and his advisors took a radically different approach to the problem than the Hoover administration. Republicans, like Hoover, approached the issues of poverty and unemployment in a Social Darwinist manner, believing that the misfortunes of the poor must have come about through some fault of their own and that they should work out those misfortunes on their own. In contrast, FDR approached the problem by changing the way the government interacted with the economy. He signed a package of legislation into law that was called the New Deal. This New Deal empowered government agencies to regulate banks and businesses, create jobs through public works, and provide welfare programs for those who needed help.

One of the very first issues that FDR addressed upon taking office in 1933 was the problem of bank closures. He called a "bank holiday," declaring all banks in the United States closed for business until the government could determine which ones were financially sound. This bank holiday lasted about a week, after which 90% of America's banks were allowed to re-open and were guaranteed to be financially healthy. However, to prevent more bank closures, the Federal Deposit Insurance Corporation (FDIC) was established in June 1933. This meant that if anyone deposited their money in a bank that later closed, the federal government would reimburse the lost money (up to $5,000). Today, that limit is $250,000.

Additionally, Congress created the Securities and Exchange Commission (SEC) in 1934 to regulate the stock market. The SEC cannot prevent the stock market from crashing. However, it makes sure that the stock market is protected from unfair practices and that those who participate in such practices are prosecuted.

Another major part of the New Deal was government spending on public works—big projects that everyone gets to use, like bridges, roads, or national parks—to create jobs for people. Numerous government agencies provided work for jobless Americans, thanks to the New Deal.

ELEANOR ROOSEVELT AT A WPA SITE IN DES MOINES, IOWA, 1936

The day before he signed the Fair Labor Standards Act in 1938, President Roosevelt remarked, "Except perhaps for the Social Security Act, it is the most far-reaching, far-sighted program for the benefit of workers ever adopted here or in any other country." This federal legislation was the first to establish a minimum wage, set a standard workweek, require overtime pay, and outlaw child labor that managed to stand up to the Supreme Court's scrutiny.

The cornerstone of the New Deal was the Social Security Act of 1935. This legislation resulted in working people having a little money taken out of their paychecks. This money would then go into the government's Social Security fund. From there, it would then be used to provide financial help for the disabled, the elderly, widows, and others who needed assistance. The idea is that you pay into the system now, so that when you retire or if some misfortune befalls you, you'll get payments that will come from future workers' checks. It's like an insurance policy against poverty and is still around today.

The New Deal made great strides in helping Americans survive the Great Depression, though it did not completely end it. By 1937, unemployment had gone down to about 14%. It was ultimately the demand for war materials created by World War II that ended the Great Depression.

More important, the New Deal marked a turning point in US history, because it represented a new involvement by the government in people's daily lives. This involvement would increase further as the 20th century progressed.

Attention Shifts Abroad

The Great Depression was not an isolated American event. Because the world's economies had become dependent on one another, one country's economic problems would spread to the others. As a result of the Great Depression in the United States, economies in Europe quickly became depressed as well.

Germany's economy in particular was not doing well. As a result of World War I, Germany relied on US loans to prop up its economy and allow it to make reparations payments to France. Once the Great Depression hit in 1929, these loans were no longer available, and the results were disastrous for Germany. By 1933, roughly a third of Germans were unemployed. The German government could not figure out how to respond to the problem, which allowed Adolf Hitler to legally come to power.

As the leader of the Nazi Party, one of Hitler's goals was to gain what he called "living space" for the German people. This led Germany to take over or invade much of eastern and northern Europe. Hitler also emphasized what came to be known as the "Final Solution." This was a plan to first relocate, and later kill, ethnic and religious Jews, plus other people the Nazis considered to be inferior, such as LGBTQ people, the mentally ill, and the Romani people (often incorrectly called "gypsies").

A similar totalitarian dictator, Benito Mussolini, had taken over Italy's government in the 1920s. Italy also had expansionist goals, leading it to invade countries such as Ethiopia and Albania. Meanwhile, military leaders had taken control of Japan and were invading East Asian sites such as Manchuria and Nanjing.

Western European countries initially responded to this aggression with a policy called appeasement. Essentially, they hoped that the Axis countries—as Germany, Italy, and Japan would come to be known—would be satisfied with what they had taken and stop. Meanwhile, just as it had in World War I, America declared itself to be officially neutral with a series of Neutrality Acts between 1935 and 1937.

World War II officially began when Great Britain and France declared war on September 3, 1939, two days after Germany invaded Poland. Although most Americans were against involvement in the developing war, FDR was not. President Roosevelt sought ways to support the Allies even though the United States still technically remained neutral, which drew the country into this war much more quickly than had happened with World War I.

World War II

The United States was able to officially stay out of the war for about two years, but once again, cultural ties linked the country to the Allies—Great Britain, France, and eventually the Soviet Union. FDR and Congress were crafty in coming up with ways to send aid to the British despite declared US neutrality. The Lend-Lease Act of 1941, for instance, allowed the United States to loan (not sell) food and war materials to Great Britain, China, and the Soviets. (France had already fallen to the Nazis at that point.)

Meanwhile, the United States tried to limit Japan's attempts at expansion in the Pacific with a series of trade restrictions, including an oil embargo, or a ban on trade. In retaliation, Japan attacked the naval base at Pearl Harbor, Hawaii, on December 7, 1941, resulting in a US declaration of war the very next day.

ALLIED TROOPS LANDING IN NORMANDY, FRANCE, ON D-DAY, JUNE 6, 1944

American troops fought mainly in two areas during World War II: in Western Europe against Germany and Italy, and in the Pacific against Japan. American troops joined the Allies in the invasions of Sicily and Italy in August 1943 to defeat Mussolini, who surrendered on September 8.

The next year, on June 6, 1944, British and American troops launched an invasion of Nazi-held France, called D-Day. General Dwight D. Eisenhower commanded the successful military operation, which allowed Allied troops to liberate France. They then worked their way eastward through Belgium toward Hitler's stronghold in Berlin, Germany. At the same time, Soviet troops were heading toward Berlin from the opposite direction. The Soviets arrived first and defeated the Germans in the Battle of Berlin, which led to the official German surrender on May 8, 1945.

The fighting in the Pacific Ocean was primarily composed of naval battles. The combatants were fighting for control of hundreds of tiny little islands. Admiral Chester W. Nimitz and General Douglas MacArthur, the commanders of the Allied forces in the Pacific, used strategies called "island-hopping" and "leap-frogging." These allowed them to take over certain islands and then use them to gain control of the territories around them, rather than having to capture every Japan-held island along their way to mainland Japan. The United States took the offensive in the Pacific in 1942 after the Battle of Midway. Once the Allies had gained control of the ocean territory around Japan, they began bombing the islands of Japan itself in 1944.

The United States had a new president, Harry S. Truman, who had succeeded Roosevelt when Roosevelt died suddenly of a brain hemorrhage in April 1945. Nuclear weapons had recently been developed through a research initiative called the Manhattan Project. President Truman decided to use the new weapons to force Japan to surrender.

The United States dropped one atomic bomb on the Japanese city of Hiroshima on August 6, 1945, and a second bomb on Nagasaki on August 9, 1945. These bombs were unlike any that came before them, creating widespread damage, not just from their blasts, but from heat and radioactivity as well. As a result, Japan formally surrendered on August 15, 1945, bringing an end to World War II.

MATTER OF CHOICE: ATOMIC BOMB

In mid-1944, the United States had begun strategically bombing Japanese cities to force Japan to surrender. In March 1945, US warplanes dropped 2,000 tons of conventional bombs on Tokyo, burning 16 square miles of the city and killing about 100,000 civilians. Still, the Japanese did not surrender. President Truman had to decide between a ground invasion or using the recently developed nuclear weapons. He argued that a ground invasion would "be opposed not only by the available organized military forces of the Empire, but also by a fanatically hostile population." He believed that using the bombs would save American lives that would have been lost in a land invasion. Instead, the two nuclear weapons dropped by the Allies cost more than 200,000 Japanese civilian lives, either immediately as a result of the bombs, or later as a result of radiation poisoning. The United States was the first and is the only country to use atomic weapons during war.

Now that the war was over, world leaders were determined not to make the same mistakes they had made at the end of World War I. Unfortunately, they made a completely different set of mistakes, leading to an era of competition between the United States and the Soviet Union called the Cold War. Major changes would take place on US soil as well, some as a result of the fear brought on by the Cold War, and others stemming from social movements that had begun decades earlier.

CHAPTER 4

PEACE AND PROXY WARS

In the aftermath of World War II, the United States and its allies attempted to establish a peace that would promote global political and economic interests. However, the United States and the Soviet Union didn't exactly agree on what those interests were, which created a new type of conflict that would shape the rest of the 20th century.

When They Came Home

While the Allies had been fighting overseas, the people at home were also working in different ways to support the war effort. Society's expectations about the type of work that white, middle- and upper-class women could do changed temporarily. Meanwhile, Black Americans had served their country at war and expected to be treated with respect for their service. So, when the veterans returned home, hoping to resume their former roles, tensions arose that eventually led to societal upheaval.

In 1939, when World War II began in Europe and the United States had declared itself neutral, American unemployment was around 17%. Although FDR's New Deal had helped, many people were still suffering from the effects of the Great Depression. When the war created a demand for armaments, Americans jumped at the chance to work in factories producing weapons and supplies to sell to the Allies. These types of industrial jobs traditionally went to men, but after the United States declared war in late 1941 and many men were sent into battle, women took their place in the factories.

Government propaganda campaigns actually urged women to take the factory jobs that the men had vacated. In fact, the famous "Rosie the Riveter—We Can Do It!" poster was the product of a World War II propaganda campaign. Other slogans called for "girls with star-spangled hearts" to join special auxiliary units of the military (since women weren't allowed in combat). In these units, women did noncombat work, like nursing, performing administrative tasks, driving, and doing mechanical work, which freed up men for combat. Some, like the Women Airforce Service Pilots (WASPs), even undertook dangerous missions, such as flying newly manufactured planes from factories to military bases. These types of jobs were mostly available only to white women, though 6,500 Black women also served in the Women's Army Auxiliary Corps (WAAC). Black women in the WAAC were usually required to serve on US soil. Only one Black battalion, the 6888th, was allowed overseas.

Though wartime is certainly scary, it also represented a real period of opportunity for white, middle-class women. It had not previously been considered proper for middle- or upper-class women to work outside the home. The work these women did during the war was, to many of them, much more fulfilling than their roles at home. Unfortunately, women of color were largely excluded from these high-paying factory jobs because of institutional racism. This is a form of racism that exists across society and in organizations. These women were relegated to domestic work as maids and nannies or the menial, lower-paying factory jobs to which women had historically had access.

Black people were also eager to support their country. About one million Black men served in the armed forces during World War II. These troops were officially segregated, with Black men serving under white officers and earning less than white servicemen.

Several all-Black units earned distinction during World War II. The Tuskegee Airmen were a specially trained all-Black pilot squadron. This elite group flew more than 15,000 extremely dangerous missions during the war, losing only 66 men in the process. Another group, nicknamed the "Buffalo Soldiers," was one of the only units of Black men to go into combat in World War II. Seven of its members earned Congressional medals of honor for their service (though not until 1997).

MATTER OF CHOICE:
EXECUTIVE ORDER 9981

Harry S. Truman was born in a former Confederate state and grew up supporting segregation, yet he became the first US president since Reconstruction to increase civil rights for Black people. Prior to the election of 1948, Democratic election strategists convinced Truman that he needed the Black vote, and according to the "Declaration of Negro Voters," a document presented by the National Association for the Advancement of Colored People (NAACP), he would need to desegregate the armed forces to get that. Civil rights leader A. Philip Randolph also pressed for military desegregation, promising that if it didn't happen, Black people would resist the draft. As a result, President Truman signed Executive Order 9981 in 1948, officially desegregating the armed forces and setting the stage for the coming civil rights movement of the 1950s and 1960s.

Black women served in the war, too. Only the Women's Army Corps allowed Black women to join, and then only one unit was allowed to serve overseas: the 6888th Central Postal Directory Battalion. The women were first sent to Birmingham, England, where they sorted through an entire building stacked to the ceiling with letters and care packages meant for soldiers. The "Six-Triple-Eight" finished its task in half the time expected and was then "rewarded" with more of the same type of work in Rouen, France, eventually making it to Paris.

In 1941, during his "Four Freedoms" speech, President Roosevelt explained why America needed to support the

Allies in Europe. He asserted that the basic things people living in a democracy could expect were "equality of opportunity . . . [and] the ending of special privilege for the few." Yet Black Americans who had worked hard to support their country during the war returned to the same discrimination and segregation that they had left.

Here was a contradiction: The United States had been fighting for freedom for people in other countries, yet it didn't extend those same freedoms to all of its own people. Black Americans; women; Mexican Americans; Indigenous peoples; Asian Americans; and lesbian, gay, bisexual, transgender, and queer/questioning (LGBTQ) people—all kinds of groups that had been discriminated against—prepared to fight.

A Time to Rebuild

When we think of the aftermaths of wars, we tend to think of big-picture, whole-country stuff—like winners and losers, treaties and territory, new flags, and changed maps. Those things are certainly prominent features of postwar periods, but wars affect the lives of ordinary people, too. Homes, schools, churches, post offices, stores, government offices, buses, and streets were destroyed throughout Europe, Africa, and the Pacific, which meant that economies were also in distress. Unfortunately, extreme political ideologies are often attractive to people who see no other options.

FDR and British Prime Minister Winston Churchill were determined to rebuild healthy economies. They believed that healthy economies would promote peace and democracy because people who have what they need are less likely to fight over resources or wage war. To make that happen, the leaders of the Allied countries started having conferences before the war was even over to discuss their postwar strategies.

A YOUNG BOY HOLDS A STUFFED ANIMAL AFTER THE GERMAN BOMBING OF LONDON, 1945

At the Yalta Conference, held in February 1945, President Roosevelt, Churchill, and Soviet Premier Joseph Stalin decided to establish a new international organization to promote peace, the United Nations. Additionally, they supported self-determination for all the countries of Europe, meaning that once the war ended, the people of every nation would be allowed to decide for themselves what kind of government they preferred.

In July 1945, the "Big Three" leaders—with new American President Harry S. Truman replacing Roosevelt, who had passed away in April—met at the Potsdam Conference. The Allies had just achieved victory in Europe in May, and they divided Germany into zones for occupation. The Soviets were the only ones bent on payments for damages caused during the war. They promised to take these reparations exclusively from their own zone and only in the form of labor or industrial goods. The leaders also agreed to conduct trials for Nazi and Japanese war criminals.

Japan had not yet been defeated, but President Truman let the other leaders know that the United States now possessed nuclear weapons and would use them on Japan if necessary. Overall, the Potsdam Conference was a lot more tense than the Yalta Conference had been. Stalin and Truman did not have a great rapport. Also, it was starting to look like the Soviets were planning to interfere in the establishment of new governments in Eastern European countries like Poland and Czechoslovakia, breaking the self-determination promise they had made at Yalta.

After Japan surrendered in August 1945, American General Douglas MacArthur was tasked with leading the occupation and rebuilding efforts. To keep the peace, he strengthened the economy by promoting landownership for farmers and labor union membership for industrial workers. To make Japan more of a republic, he drafted a new constitution that drew power away from the emperor and focused on a parliament. This constitution also gave equal rights to women, recognized numerous civil liberties, and forbade Japan to make war. This same premise would work well in Western Europe, too.

The Marshall Plan and the Truman Doctrine

Historically, wars tend to happen more often in times of famine. This makes sense; people are more likely get into disputes if there are not enough resources to go around. Just after World War II, this was definitely the case in Europe, which faced food scarcities, huge national debts, currency issues, and physical damage to homes and workplaces.

Enter the Marshall Plan, named for George C. Marshall, who had been a general in World War II and was now President Truman's secretary of state. In 1947, he described his plan to rebuild Europe. Essentially, the United States would first offer money to European nations for food and fuel, and later it would help them rebuild cities and industry. In exchange, participating European countries would commit to work together to draft a plan for economic recovery, collaborate to ensure the economic health of all member countries, and reduce trade barriers among themselves. This would eventually evolve into the modern European Union.

The offer was made to all European countries, including the Soviet Union and its satellites, but Stalin refused, saying it was an attempt at American imperialism. In 1948, Congress approved a total of $12 billion in aid to 17 European nations. About half of the continent—the Soviet Union, its satellites, Yugoslavia, Finland, Albania, and Spain—did not receive aid. By 1952, when the plan ended, all 17 countries that had received aid experienced between 15% and 25% growth in their gross domestic products (GDP), a measure of economic health.

The Marshall Plan is considered a turning point in US foreign policy. For the first time after a major war, the United States was not simply retreating back to isolationism. Instead, it was promoting *future* international stability. This showed that the United States' place in the world order had changed. It had become a global superpower—a sort of "boss country" that dominated international relations.

One goal of the Marshall Plan had been to simply prevent war from reoccurring. Another goal was to prevent the spread of communism through Western Europe. Because the Soviet Union had broken the promise it had made at the Yalta Conference to allow the countries of Eastern Europe to choose their own forms of government, US leaders worried that the Soviet Union might make further attempts to expand.

A PRO-MARSHALL PLAN DEMONSTRATION IN GERMANY, 1948

But why would the USSR do such a thing if it would
threaten an already fragile relationship with the United
States? The Soviet Union had been invaded by Germany twice
in the 20th century. Stalin was particularly worried about
the nation's military security. He used the Soviet military to
create a buffer zone of satellite countries between the USSR
and Germany. Satellite nations were technically independent,
but forced to maintain communist governments that followed
Soviet-approved policies. These satellite nations were East
Germany, Czechoslovakia, Poland, Albania, Romania, Bulgaria,
and Hungary.

By 1947, the Soviet Union appeared to be spreading
communism all over Eastern Europe. China was also fighting
a civil war of communists versus nationalists (and the communists would soon win). Meanwhile, a communist leader
named Josip Broz Tito had taken over Yugoslavia (a country

in southeastern Europe). Communists were also trying to overthrow the governments of Greece and Turkey. While US leaders wanted to take action, they did not want to engage in military interventions so soon after World War II was over.

President Truman pledged that, in conflicts between communists and non-communists, the United States would always support the non-communist side. This policy of containment, which aimed to prevent the spread of communism, became known as the Truman Doctrine. This strategy essentially dictated international relations for the United States for the next 30 years or so. Anywhere communists tried to take over, the United States would get involved *somehow*—by sending money, troops, weapons, spies, nuclear information, and the like to the non-communist side. The Soviet Union and China took the opposite approach by supporting the communists.

Overall, the Allies succeeded in promoting Western Europe's economic health and cooperation with the Marshall Plan. While managing to avoid the mistakes they had made after World War I, however, they made other mistakes that led to a totally different kind of war.

The Cold War, NATO, and the Warsaw Pact

The most direct political effect of World War II was the Cold War. A cold war results when opposing countries find economic and diplomatic ways to strike at each other. They might refuse to trade with each other, convince other countries to form alliances with them, or get involved with hostilities between other countries.

The Cold War came about due to the countries' differing goals after the war. The Soviet Union was concerned with its own military security, so it established the satellite nations in violation of the agreement that Stalin had made at the Yalta Conference to grant self-determination to the people of Europe. On the other hand, the main postwar goal of the United States was to promote healthy economies to encourage the growth of democracy. This served as the impetus, or motivation, for the Marshall Plan, the Truman Doctrine, and monetary aid to Greece and Turkey. These actions did not sit well with the Soviet Union. President Truman now viewed Stalin as hostile and untrustworthy. Meanwhile, the United States had nuclear weapons, and Truman had proven to the world that he was more than ready to use them.

UP FOR DEBATE: WHO STARTED THE COLD WAR?

Traditionally, American historians put the blame on Stalin for having initiated the Cold War. He *did* sign the Declaration of Liberated Europe at the Yalta Conference, stating that the Allies would "enable the liberated peoples . . . to create democratic institutions of their own choice." His use of Soviet military pressure to establish satellite nations in Eastern Europe just after World War II absolutely violated that promise and led to distrust between the two countries. But revisionist historians point out that President Truman and the United States should shoulder some of the blame as well. Some say that Stalin planned to be cooperative, but he saw the Marshall Plan and Truman Doctrine as attempts by the United States to use its economic power to dominate Europe.

A GROUP OF GERMAN CHILDREN STAND ON BUILDING RUBBLE, CHEERING A UNITED STATES CARGO AIRPLANE AS IT FLIES OVER A WESTERN SECTION OF BERLIN, 1948

By 1948, some real pent-up hostility had built up between the two countries. Then Stalin tried to cut off railroad and automobile access to West Berlin, a free city in East Germany, thinking that if he cut off its supplies, the Allies would allow him to take control of the city. However, the policy of containing communism would not allow that. So for 10 months, US and British pilots airlifted supplies to West Berliners until Stalin gave up and lifted the blockade in May 1949. Containment succeeded, and West Berlin remained free.

The Berlin Blockade made the Union of Soviet Socialist Republics, also known as the USSR, seem even more volatile, unpredictable, and untrustworthy. In April 1949, the United States, Canada, Great Britain, and nine other Western European countries formed the North Atlantic Treaty Organization (NATO), a defense alliance. Its founding treaty stated that "an armed attack against one or more [member nations] shall be considered an attack against them all."

The Soviet Union responded by officially forming its own defense alliance, composed of itself and its satellites, through the Warsaw Pact in 1955. Now the world's dominant countries and their allies were neatly divided into two opposing camps for the purpose of military defense. This implied that the world powers were expecting some kind of war to happen at any moment. Countries were on edge, and this sense dominated politics for the next 35 years or so.

Cold War Hotspots: Korea, Iran, Vietnam, and Cuba

Several Cold War issues stirred up that edgy feeling in global politics in the 1950s and early 1960s. US and Soviet interests in the politics of Korea, Iran, Vietnam, and Cuba caused a few "hot wars," or wars with active military involvement, and brought the United States to the brink of nuclear war.

The Korean War

During World War II, Korea had been occupied by Japan. After the war ended, it was divided in half, at the 38th parallel (a line of latitude). Soviet troops were to occupy the northern half and US troops were to occupy the southern half. In 1948, the Soviet Union supported the establishment of a Korean communist government led by Kim Il-Sung in the north. Meanwhile, the United States and United Nations arranged for elections that resulted in the establishment of the Republic of Korea in the south.

In 1950, North Korea invaded South Korea, intending to unite the country under communist rule. Communist China openly supported the North Koreans, while the Soviet Union did so in secret. The Truman Doctrine would not allow the

United States to leave this alone, so US troops began arriving to support the South Koreans, creating a proxy war. A proxy is a substitute, or stand-in, so in a proxy war, two countries who are not officially at war find two countries who *are* fighting and support them.

In 1953, North and South Korea signed an armistice, an agreement to stop fighting. North Korea remained communist, and South Korea remained non-communist, so containment was successful. More important, the United States had shown the USSR that it was serious about not allowing communism to spread. At home, many Americans were confused about why the United States had been involved in such a faraway war that didn't seem to have anything to do with them, so the Korean War was extremely unpopular.

Operation Ajax

In 1908, a British company discovered oil in Iran, which was then called Persia, allowing Great Britain to maintain economic control over Iran's growing oil resources until 1951. In that year, Mohammad Mossadegh was elected to the role of Iranian prime minister. Mossadegh was a nationalist, meaning that he wanted to get rid of foreign influences on Iran and initiate more self-government. He also wanted to limit British control over the Iranian oil fields, but the British refused to cooperate. As a result, the Iranian Parliament voted to completely expel the British. In retaliation, the British organized a worldwide boycott of Iranian oil.

Concerned about the loss of British investors' profits, Prime Minister Churchill requested help from the Eisenhower administration to overthrow Mossadegh. The US government feared that Iran would remain unstable under Mossadegh due to the economic problems created by the oil boycott, and the Soviets would try to take over. Framing the situation in Iran as an issue of containment, President

Eisenhower approved a plan for the US Central Intelligence Agency (CIA) to purposely diminish support for Mossadegh, called "Operation Ajax."

CIA agents hired Iranian rioters, distributed advertisements attacking Mossadegh, and paid mercenaries (hired soldiers) to imprison Mossadegh. In his place, the former ruler of Iran—the shah, or king—returned to power. He pledged to provide access to Iranian oil in return for support from the US government. The shah was considered to be a dictator, and the fact that the United States had backed him in replacing the democratically elected Mossadegh caused animosity toward the United States among Iranian people.

Origins of the Vietnam War

Just one year after the Korean War armistice in 1954, similar problems cropped up in Indochina, or modern-day Vietnam. Before World War II, Indochina had been a French colony, but it had been occupied by Japan during the war. After the war, the French tried to occupy it again. The Vietnamese opposed that, causing a nationalist revolt. The United States' ally, France, was out of money and needed help, so the country once again got entangled in another Asian proxy war that was unpopular among voters. We'll go into further detail about the Vietnam War in chapter 6.

Cuban Missile Crisis

The Caribbean island of Cuba was the setting of yet another Cold War showdown. Fidel Castro, a communist dictator, took over Cuba in 1959. In 1961, the United States tried to overthrow Castro but failed. Wanting to prevent future invasions, Castro agreed to allow the Soviet Union to begin building nuclear missiles on the island. In October 1962, US spy planes photographed these missile sites, setting off the Cuban Missile Crisis.

Because Cuba is just 90 miles southeast of Florida, the placement of the Soviets' missile-building sites on the island meant that the Soviet Union could easily demolish several US cities with atomic bombs. President John F. Kennedy ordered a naval quarantine of Cuba, preventing any more weapons from being delivered. Additionally, he announced that the United States would regard any nuclear attack from Cuba as an attack by the Soviet Union and respond accordingly.

For 13 days, it appeared that the world might be blown up by Soviet nukes at any moment. Finally, Kennedy and the new Soviet leader, Nikita Khrushchev (Stalin had died in 1953), agreed that the Soviets would remove their missiles if the United States would remove missiles it had stationed in Turkey. Thus, the crisis ended on October 28, 1962.

The Cuban Missile Crisis was the closest the world has ever come to full-scale nuclear war. In 1962, both the United States and the Soviet Union had enough nukes to create a situation called "mutually assured destruction." Essentially, one side drops an atomic bomb and the other side retaliates, and then the first side bombs back, and this goes on until the entire world is destroyed. Fortunately, in the latter part of the 20th century, both countries agreed to dramatically reduce their stockpiles of weapons to make nuclear war far less likely in the future.

The Space Race

The Cold War competition between the Soviet Union and the United States was so intense that it even extended into *space*. In 1957, the Soviet Union launched *Sputnik*, which was the first artificial satellite to orbit the Earth. The United States had also been planning to launch a satellite into space, but at that time, it had only developed a rocket that could launch a satellite. When the news of *Sputnik*'s launch reached US officials, they became alarmed. This marked the beginning of the "Space Race," a period of competition for space technology between the two countries.

The launch of *Vanguard*, the first US satellite, in December 1957 was a huge failure. The satellite rose a mere four feet in the air before exploding. So, in January 1958, the United States set up a new government agency, the National Aeronautics and Space Administration (NASA), to conduct space research. The Soviet Union was able to get a dog to orbit the Earth on its second satellite before the United States even got its first successful satellite, *Explorer 1*, into space in 1958. The USSR was also the first to get people into space and to conduct a space walk. However, the United States took the lead in 1969, when Neil Armstrong and Buzz Aldrin became the first humans to walk on the moon.

FOCUS POINT: THE NATIONAL DEFENSE EDUCATION ACT

Once the Space Race began and it became clear that the Soviet Union was winning, US government officials began to worry that the country was not producing enough highly qualified scientists and engineers. The National Defense Education Act (NDEA) was passed in 1958 to increase funding for higher education programs, most notably making low-interest loans available to students who wanted to enroll in college mathematics, science, or engineering programs. Congress extended the NDEA program until 1970 and voted to increase its funding several times. The funds contributed in part to a modest increase in US educational attainment.

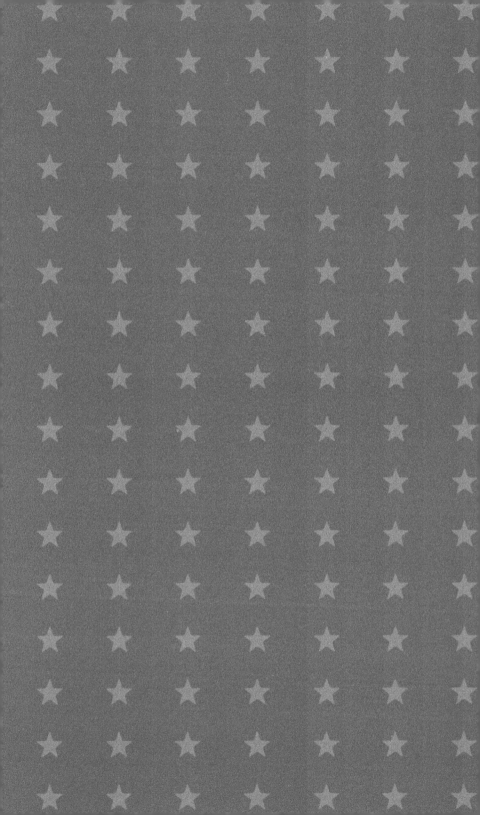

CHAPTER 5
THE "GOLDEN" 1950s

Many people think of the 1950s as an idyllic era, when everyone went down to the local diner during their free time. Virtuous ponytailed girls and well-mannered young men in letter jackets shared milkshakes with two straws, while immaculately dressed adults ate pie and bantered with waitresses named "Flo" and "Jolene." This idea of the 1950s as the "good ol' days" probably stems from its status as a period of relative economic prosperity. The decade was also a time of conformity and focus on the family unit. As with all periods of prosperity, not all groups benefitted, and an emphasis on conformity usually leads to trouble for those who refuse to conform or are perceived as not conforming.

The Golden Age of Capitalism

Though Franklin D. Roosevelt's New Deal helped lessen the pain of the Great Depression, it was World War II that really brought it to an end. The war created demand for all the items needed for battle: guns, bullets, tanks, uniforms, canned food, and so much more. Even before the United States got officially involved in the war, it was providing those supplies to the Allies. In 1939, when World War II began, US unemployment was close to 15%, but by 1944, one year before the war ended, it had dropped to the record low of 1%. Even after the war, during the second half of the 1940s and all of the 1950s, the economy boomed.

One factor that contributed to this prosperity was government spending. Concerned that those who had been serving in the military would become unemployed when the war was over, FDR signed the Servicemen's Readjustment Act, known today as the GI Bill, into law. This allowed veterans to access unemployment insurance while they looked for work, tuition assistance to enroll in job training or college, and low-interest loans to buy homes. Other government agencies created during the New Deal, such as the Federal Housing Authority (FHA), provided mortgage loans to non-veterans, making it easier for other Americans to buy homes.

The Federal Aid Highway Act of 1956 also boosted the economy. Its 41,000 miles of organized highway roads made driving around the United States much easier and stimulated the automobile and construction industries. The unfolding events of the Cold War additionally resulted in more military spending, leading to the development of what is often referred to as the "military-industrial complex." This refers to a large web of private companies that have contracts with the military to produce weapons and other goods that the military might need.

MEN WORKING ON MACHINES AT THE NEW YORK METROPOLITAN TECHNICAL SCHOOL, 1940S–'50S

So-called "pent-up demand" also contributed to the economic boom. Basically, people had felt deprived during the war. Many items had either been rationed or unavailable, and the government had encouraged people to put their money into savings bonds. Now that the war was over, consumers had money to spend, and items that had been previously unavailable had become available again, so they splurged. The invention of the credit card in 1950 made extra spending even easier.

Of course, this affluence was not available to everyone. Racism and discrimination made it much more difficult for Black people and immigrants to access the high-paying jobs that would have allowed them to own homes and purchase expensive consumer goods. For example, in 1959, 55% of Black families lived below the poverty line, while just 18% of white families were considered poor.

Babies in the 'Burbs

One interesting effect of the end of World War II was the baby boom. Between 1946 and 1964, the birth rate in the United States increased significantly. Information from the National Center for Health Statistics illustrates just how much the birth rate increased. In 1940, the average number of children per woman in the United States was 2.3; by 1950 the average had grown to 3.1, and by 1960, it was 3.7.

Thousands of soldiers in their early 20s had returned from war and were eager to be reunited with their sweethearts, get married, and start families. That was definitely part of the cause for the baby boom. Considering the changing economic conditions after the war will help us understand why these returning soldiers were able to start families so quickly.

When the economy is not doing well, the birth rate tends to fall. For example, between 1920 and 1940, which included the Great Depression, the average number of children per woman fell from 3.3 to 2.3. This happens because people do not eat as well, and poor nutrition affects women's ability to bear children. Additionally, young couples tend to delay marriage and put off having children. But because the US economy was so prosperous after World War II, young men were able to find jobs and affordable housing, so they got married and had children earlier, leading to the baby boom.

This led to the birth of the suburbs. After all, these new families had to live somewhere. William Levitt, who had put up military housing with the navy during World War II using assembly line processes, thought the same techniques could be applied to building houses for returning veterans. He convinced his father, who owned a construction company, to try it out. Thus, the first mass-produced suburban neighborhoods were built. To cut costs, the Levitts limited choices within their neighborhoods. There were only two or three floorplans and two colors of paint to choose from. This meant that houses looked very similar. "Levittown" was very popular, and soon other housing developers began imitating that model.

Life in the suburbs was almost exclusively limited to white families. Levitt had restrictions written into the contracts for his neighborhoods that houses would not be sold to Black families. Federal housing agencies created maps of neighborhoods and color-coded them according to their general desirability and the credit-worthiness of their inhabitants. Neighborhoods where Black people and other people of color lived were outlined in red, so this practice was called "redlining."

A NEW HOUSING DEVELOPMENT UNDER CONSTRUCTION IN ARLINGTON HEIGHTS, ILLINOIS, CIRCA 1954

Banks refused to give loans to people who lived in redlined communities and wanted to make improvements to their properties or move to other neighborhoods. This kind of institutional racism resulted in de facto segregation—segregation that is not legally required, but happens as a result of policies and practices.

About 80% of workers who lived in the suburbs commuted to the city to work, which meant they needed cars. In 1940, about 27 million cars were on the roads in the United States. By 1950, that number had risen to 40 million. Cars became an important status symbol and were considered a necessity in the suburbs. New societal patterns related to "car culture" began to appear: Families ate at fast-food restaurants like McDonald's, went to drive-in movies, and traveled more frequently on road trips, stopping to rest at motels like Howard Johnson's.

UP FOR DEBATE: THE GOOD OL' DAYS?

Some baby boomers wax nostalgic for the "good ol' days" of the 1950s, when it seemed like the economy was booming and happy families lived in orderly suburbs. There was even a TV show in the 1970s called *Happy Days* based on this very theme. However, some aspects of the 1950s were not so idyllic. Taxes were very high, racism and sexism were prevalent, and the standard of living that even middle-class white families could expect was much lower than they enjoy today.

The baby boom caused a cultural focus on children and mothering, so expectations for women in the home increased greatly. The middle-class suburban mother was considered the ideal, but life in the suburbs could be isolating for mothers, who were now removed from traditional sources of support like grandparents and other family members. Suburban mothers often spent much of their time driving their children to and from various activities and had few sources of social or intellectual stimulation. Men spent much of their time commuting to work and working, so they were rarely home and did not contribute much to childcare or domestic chores.

These expectations were passed on to poorer women as well. Their husbands' jobs might not pay well enough for these women to forgo working, so they might have to balance the increased demands of parenting and housekeeping with some outside work—usually low-paying domestic jobs or factory work. Many women were becoming dissatisfied with their roles as mothers first and longed for some way to express their individuality. This would eventually lead to the women's movement of the 1960s.

The baby boom continued to affect the 20th and 21st centuries as the "boomers" got older. When they grew to school age, they required increased funding for schools. When they became teenagers, their preferences for clothing and music dominated popular culture. Most boomers are now senior citizens, a unique generation of people who are living longer than any other generation of Americans ever has, with their own needs for specialized housing and products.

TVs and Tunes

After reading about the growth of the suburbs after World War II, it's easy to imagine that idyllic suburban family gathered around the TV on a stylish couch in a pristine living room. In fact, TVs did become widely available in the early 1950s. The postwar economic boom made it possible for more families to afford televisions, and by 1955 more than half of American families owned one.

Most TV shows in the 1950s reflected the conservative family values and conformity that is usually associated with the time period. Programs like *Leave it to Beaver* and *Father Knows Best* centered on a white middle-class family with a father who left every morning for work wearing a suit and carrying a briefcase. A beautifully dressed mother in high heels and lipstick stood on the porch and kissed him and the two polite, well-groomed children goodbye. She then stayed home all day, cleaning the house and cooking. Usually, the plot revolved around a moral problem that could be easily solved with a short heart-to-heart family conference at the end of the episode.

Only rare shows, such as *Gunsmoke*, a Western, dealt with controversial issues. Television programs infrequently showed ethnic minorities or reflected the 25% of American families living in poverty. For the most part, the demographic makeup of the nation was not reflected on TV.

The advent of nationwide television programs helped create a uniform national culture. Americans grew increasingly familiar with the same television characters who promoted specific fashions, lifestyles, and values. Advertisements for name-brand products created psychological "needs." Regional accents began to slowly subside as television viewers were exposed to standardized versions of spoken English. As more and more households began to own televisions in the

1960s and 1970s and programming increased in the 1980s and 1990s, American cities, towns, and regions became even more similar to one another.

Before the spread of televisions, most people had gotten their entertainment from the radio. Radio had featured all kinds of programming, including dramas, comedies, and news shows. Once TV's popularity grew, radio began to focus on music to keep people listening.

In the early 1950s, the music of Black blues singers from Chicago, such as Muddy Waters and B. B. King, became popular among both Black and white teenagers. Some radio stations called it "race music" and banned it, but other stations capitalized on its popularity. A disc jockey named Alan Freed began referring to the music as "rock 'n' roll" and played artists such as Little Richard and Chuck Berry on his late-night radio program.

Rock 'n' roll was already bringing Black and white audiences together when Elvis Presley came along. A white singer who sang songs written by Black artists, Elvis blended blues, rock 'n' roll, country, and gospel music. In his TV appearances, he sang and gyrated his hips suggestively. The teenagers went wild! However, older audiences found his dancing to be inappropriate for young people. Just as it is now, adult disfavor is always the very best way to cement teenagers' approval. In this way, television made Elvis the first rock 'n' roll icon.

The Civil Rights Movement

While rock 'n' roll may have brought Black and white teenagers together at record shops and concerts, it took more than a new musical genre to end segregation.

Black Americans who moved north during the Great Migration still faced racism. Many cities used policies that confined Black people to certain neighborhoods and made it difficult for them to purchase homes, even within those neighborhoods. Additionally, Black people were often barred from joining unions and were forced to take the lowest-paying and most dangerous jobs.

Just as World War I had, World War II created more factory work. Black workers were still eager to work in the war industry but did not want to continue to be subjected to the same racist policies. About 1.2 million Black Americans fought in World War II, which was supposedly a fight for freedom and democracy, and against tyranny and racism. This seemed very hypocritical, since Black Americans were still subject to discrimination and segregation at home. In this way, World War II set the stage for the civil rights movement of the 1950s and 1960s.

One prominent organization that fought for civil rights was the National Association for the Advancement of Colored People (NAACP). As the chief counsel (lawyer) for the NAACP, Thurgood Marshall challenged various segregationist policies through court cases in the late 1940s and early 1950s. The most important of these was *Brown v. Board of Education*. In this 1954 case, the Supreme Court ruled that segregation in schools was not constitutional because it violated the equal protection clause of the Fourteenth Amendment, and that being segregated made Black children feel inferior, causing psychological damage.

This landmark court decision was followed by *Brown v. Board of Education II*, in which the Supreme Court made it difficult to enforce their own previous decision. *Brown II*, as it is called, put district courts in charge of desegregating schools and set a time limit for desegregation: "with all deliberate speed." The problem was that district courts had been the ones to allow segregation in the first place, and "all deliberate speed" is very vague and could be interpreted to mean "later."

Black children were not the only ones who had to attend segregated schools. In the southern states, Mexican American children were also sent to separate facilities. In 1946, five Mexican families sued the Westminster School District in Orange County, California, on behalf of 5,000 students who had been segregated. The case made it to the US Court of Appeals, which is one step below the US Supreme Court. That court ruled that segregation violated the equal protection clause of the Fourteenth Amendment, just as the Supreme Court later ruled in 1954 with regard to Black students. Thurgood Marshall, one of the NAACP's attorneys, even cited this court case when making his argument for *Brown v. Board of Education.*

Two years later, in September 1957, nine Black teenagers in Little Rock, Arkansas, tried to enter Central High School to attend classes. They were met by the state's National Guard, which Governor Orval Faubus had ordered to keep the students from entering the school. Even after a federal judge ordered the National Guard to stand down and local police escorted the "Little Rock Nine" to school, a mob of angry white people harassed the students. President Eisenhower had to send 1,000 Army paratroopers to guard the students for the rest of the year. The next year, Governor Faubus closed down the high schools in Little Rock to prevent further integration. They did not reopen until the courts forced them to do so in 1959.

A SCHOOL IS INTEGRATED IN CLINTON, TENNESSEE, 1956

This kind of reaction to desegregation came to be known as "massive resistance." More than 100 Southern senators had signed an agreement called the "Southern Manifesto" in opposition to integrating schools. Southern states found ways around integration. For example, they might withhold state funds from schools that favored integration. Additionally, pupil placement laws gave local school districts authority to place students in certain schools according to characteristics not related to race (but that still managed to keep schools segregated).

The civil rights movement wasn't just about state laws and court decisions, though. It was also a grassroots movement, meaning that ordinary people worked together at the local level to create change. Probably the most iconic event of the movement was the day in 1955 when a bus driver asked Rosa Parks, a Black department store worker living in Montgomery, Alabama, to give up her seat and move to the back of the bus or be arrested. Parks' refusal and arrest kicked off the Montgomery bus boycott, which was led by a local minister, Martin Luther King Jr.

King urged his supporters to use civil disobedience, or peaceful refusal to obey unjust laws. After 13 months, the boycotters got affirmation from the Supreme Court that segregation on public buses was unconstitutional. The success of the boycott led King and others to form the Southern Christian Leadership Conference (SCLC) to continue the fight for civil rights using nonviolent protest into the 1960s.

The Red Scare of the 1950s

While to a certain extent, people in all time periods have been encouraged to conform to the accepted beliefs and values of society, the 1950s was an exceptionally conformist era. This emphasis on conformity came about in large part because of growing fear of the spread of communism—in particular, that some people within the United States were working to overthrow the government.

Americans had reason to be concerned about the threat of communism in the years after World War II. Joseph Stalin was spreading Soviet-style communism throughout Eastern Europe; the Soviet Union had developed its own atomic bombs; communists led by Mao Zedong had taken over mainland China, and American troops were being deployed to fight communists in Korea.

A special Congressional committee that had been formed in the 1930s, the House Un-American Activities Committee (HUAC) began to hold hearings of suspected communists in 1947. The committee alleged that communists working in Hollywood had been sneaking propaganda into movies. The committee would question suspects harshly and ask for the names of others they knew who might be communists. A specific group of writers and producers who refused to cooperate with HUAC, known as the "Hollywood Ten," were either jailed or "blacklisted" in the movie industry, which meant that no entertainment company would hire them.

When Americans found out that the Soviet Union had successfully developed nuclear weapons in 1949, suspicions arose about spies having revealed US nuclear secrets. Just after World War II ended, the United States and Great Britain had worked together on the VENONA project to decipher the Soviet telegraph code. This provided evidence to prosecute numerous Soviet spies. The US Federal Bureau of Investigation (FBI) questioned a British scientist named Klaus Fuchs, based on information they had found in a decoded telegram sent to the Soviet Embassy. Fuchs confessed to having worked as a Soviet spy since 1942, and he was sentenced to 14 years in prison. He also gave the FBI the names of other spies, such as Julius and Ethel Rosenberg, who were sentenced to death by electric chair for refusing to cooperate. This confirmation that actual communist spies, or "reds," were working in the United States simply made the Red Scare worse.

Republican Senator Joseph McCarthy played on these fears when, while making a speech in 1950, he claimed to know of 205 communists who were working in the US Department of State, the agency responsible for international affairs and foreign policy. The US Senate set up a special committee to investigate McCarthy's claim, later announcing that it had no merit. The Senate, however, could not decide whether to accept the report. Blaming the Democrats for being "soft on Communism," McCarthy began accusing other government agencies of harboring communists. This boosted Republican popularity and helped the party take control of the Senate and the presidency in 1952.

MATTER OF CHOICE: EISENHOWER AND MCCARTHY

Though Republican Presidential candidate Dwight Eisenhower strongly disapproved of McCarthy's sensationalist methods of rooting out communists working in the US government, he refused to publicly criticize him. When McCarthy criticized Former Secretary of State George Marshall, Eisenhower wanted to defend Marshall in a speech but chose not to because he feared that angering McCarthy's Republican supporters would hurt his chances of winning the presidential election. After he won the election, President Eisenhower continued to keep quiet on the subject of McCarthy, fearing that publicly denouncing him would only bring him more attention.

In 1953, McCarthy became the leader of the Senate Committee on Government Operations, which gave him more power to investigate supposed communists. His way of questioning suspects was widely criticized as unfair, abusive, and dishonest. He rarely produced evidence to back up his claims, and he frequently violated his witnesses' due process rights and freedom of speech. Finally, in 1954, McCarthy went too far and attacked the secretary of the army. The Army–McCarthy hearings that resulted were nationally televised. Americans saw how McCarthy treated witnesses and began to view him as a villain. In December of 1954, the Senate voted to censure McCarthy. (Censure is an official statement of disapproval but does not require the censured official to leave office.) As a result, McCarthy's power and influence declined, and he died of complications from alcoholism in 1957.

After McCarthy's downfall, a series of Supreme Court decisions began to undo some of the damage that the Red Scare had done to accused individuals. Chief Justice Earl Warren was a great promoter of civil liberties, the freedoms guaranteed to us in the Bill of Rights. Under his leadership, several McCarthy-era convictions were reversed.

Counterculture Movements: The Beats and Hippies

Not everyone agreed that prosperity would solve society's ills, that conformity was acceptable in order to achieve wealth, or that living in a middle-class suburb was ideal. In the 1950s and 1960s, counterculture movements—consisting of groups of people who opposed the status quo—rejected established social norms and created their own systems of values.

In the 1950s, a group of musicians, artists, and poets called the "Beats" rejected middle-class values and instead chose to focus on using their art to change consciousness. The name "Beat" had multiple meanings—being "beat" as in tired, "beat" in a musical sense, and as an abbreviation for "beatific," a reference to the bliss that could come from well-written poetry. To free their minds from the restrictions of society, Beats sought heightened sensory awareness through the use of drugs, jazz, and Zen Buddhism. Well-known Beat authors included Jack Kerouac, who wrote the novel *On the Road*, and Allen Ginsberg, who wrote *Howl*, an epic poem.

Considered the descendants of the Beats, "hippies" were mostly white, middle-class twenty-somethings who protested the politics and consumerism of the 1960s. They viewed the values of mainstream America as oppressive, so they refused to participate in society, seeking alternative ways to live. Some moved to "hippie hotspots" like the Haight-Ashbury district in San Francisco or the East Village in New York. Others tried sharing food, responsibilities, and living arrangements in rural communes.

In January 1967, students staged the "Human Be-In," a peaceful gathering celebrating the questioning of authority, in San Francisco's Golden Gate Park. The event attracted hordes of hippies to the San Francisco area that spring and summer, which was dubbed the "Summer of Love." In 1969, about 500,000 people traveled to rural New York for the most symbolic event of the counterculture movement: Woodstock, a three-day-long concert that included 32 performers.

Some parts of the hippie movement—particularly its protest of the Vietnam War—became irrelevant in the first half of the 1970s, as the US withdrew from the war in 1973. But the hippies have left their mark on modern life. The organic food and environmentalist movements were direct outgrowths of communal living arrangements that hippies experimented with. And if you visit a city like Austin, Texas, or Portland, Oregon, you could make the argument that the hippie movement never really ended.

CHAPTER 6

THE "RADICAL" 1960s

After the 15 or so years of relative prosperity and conservatism following World War II, the social and economic problems that had been "swept under the rug" for a while finally came to light in the 1960s. For most of the decade, Democratic Presidents John F. Kennedy and Lyndon B. Johnson strove to enact domestic reforms to create equal opportunities for all Americans. These reforms clashed with the need to address foreign policy issues resulting from the Cold War, which combined with tragic events in 1968 to end the decade with an air of disillusionment and discord.

John F. Kennedy and the "New Frontier"

John F. Kennedy accepted his nomination as the Democratic candidate for president in 1960 with a speech outlining the goals of his campaign: "We stand today on the edge of a New Frontier . . . Beyond that frontier are the uncharted areas of science and space, unsolved problems of peace and war, unconquered pockets of ignorance and prejudice, unanswered questions of poverty and surplus." Once JFK was elected, his package of economic and social reforms would be called the "New Frontier" in reference to this speech and the issues he sought to address as president.

First, though, he had to get elected. He faced Republican Richard Nixon, who had eight years of experience as President Dwight Eisenhower's vice president. Though Kennedy had served in both the House of Representatives and the Senate, he was relatively young and did not have as much political experience as Nixon did. Another potential issue was his religion; he was Catholic, and anti-Catholic attitudes had prevailed in America since the Puritans settled in New England in the 1600s. Some voters feared that a Catholic president might be dominated by the pope. The biggest issue, however, was that JFK courted Black voters in the South by supporting civil rights, which earned him the animosity of Southern Democrats.

The election was very close. JFK won by two-tenths of a percent in the popular vote, though he had a fairly comfortable lead in the Electoral College, the system by which the president is chosen by a group of electors representing the states. Once Kennedy became president, he faced a Congress controlled by conservative Democrats who stymied many of his efforts at reform. Kennedy wanted to increase federal aid to education, provide health insurance for senior citizens, protect wild land from development, and give the federal government greater power to deal with economic recessions, but he was unable to persuade Congress.

Some parts of the New Frontier did make it through Congress to become law. Most famously, Kennedy persuaded Congress to expand funding for NASA in order to land a man on the moon before the end of the decade. The Trade Expansion Act of 1962 led to decreased tariffs (import taxes) between the United States and European countries. This allowed for more international trade and fostered positive international relations. The Peace Corps arranged for American volunteers to work in underdeveloped countries to assist with education, community health, agriculture, and other areas of need. (Peace Corps volunteers still serve in 60 countries today.) Other successful policies extended the New Deal from the 1930s, such as increased Social Security benefits, an increased minimum wage, and federal grants and loans to economically disadvantaged areas such as Appalachia.

Tragically, John F. Kennedy was assassinated in Dallas, Texas on November 22, 1963. His vice president, Lyndon B. Johnson, was sworn in as president about two hours later aboard Air Force One at the Dallas airport.

UP FOR DEBATE: THE JFK ASSASSINATION

Less than one week after President Kennedy's assassination, President Lyndon B. Johnson established the Warren Commission to investigate Kennedy's death. The commission concluded that Kennedy had been shot by a lone gunman, Lee Harvey Oswald, who fired three shots from a window in the Texas Schoolbook Depository building. However, some witnesses' accounts of the attack and a home movie called the Zapruder film cast doubt upon the commission's report, leading to the proliferation of conspiracy theories.

Lyndon B. Johnson and the "Great Society"

President Johnson (LBJ) did not have JFK's personal charm or movie-star looks, but unlike Kennedy, LBJ had a special talent for maneuvering legislation through Congress. He knew that JFK's assassination had created a short moment of national unity, so he hurried to encourage Congress to pass some of Kennedy's stalled bills. Johnson was successful. The Revenue Act of 1964 created a $10 billion tax cut that stimulated the economy. Additionally, the Civil Rights Act of 1964 finally overcame opposition to outlaw segregation in public facilities.

LBJ also launched a "War on Poverty." The Economic Opportunity Act of 1964 included several long-lasting programs intended to help poor people find their way out of poverty, such as the Job Corps youth training program; Volunteers in Service to America (VISTA), a domestic version of the Peace Corps; Head Start, a preschool program; work-study programs for college students; and the Community Action Program, which created neighborhood-improvement public works projects that provided jobs for many. Each of these programs is still operating in some manner today.

After the landslide election of 1964, Johnson introduced a new package of legislation, which he called the "Great Society." This legislation sought to end poverty and racial injustice, create equal opportunities for people, and improve everyone's quality of life.

In 1945, President Harry S. Truman had proposed federal health insurance and aid to education, but both had been blocked in Congress. LBJ used his legislative savvy to get these programs enacted. The Medicare and Medicaid Act of 1965 established government-funded healthcare for the elderly and economically disadvantaged. These programs are still active today. Other accomplishments of the Great Society program included federal assistance for housing, the environment, and consumer protection.

Another significant law that resulted from this flurry of legislation was the Immigration and Naturalization Act of 1965. This law ended the quota system based on nationality that had been created in the 1920s and allowed immigrants of non-European ancestry greater access to the United States. (Remember, some immigrants, such as those from China, had been essentially barred entry to the United States since the 19th century by the Chinese Exclusion Act of 1882.)

The Great Society had many successes, but it also contributed to the growth of "big government," which conservatives did not care for, and led to a conservative backlash that would become especially strong in the 1980s. The programs created by the Great Society were very expensive, and in some cases, funds were mismanaged or went to individuals who committed welfare fraud. Additionally, the costs contributed to the national debt, which continues to be a problem.

The Vietnam War

Domestically, both Presidents Kennedy and Johnson were focused on economic and social reforms. With regard to foreign affairs, Cold War issues of containment (the policy of preventing communism from spreading) dominated their agendas. During both administrations, the conflict in Vietnam progressed, and during LBJ's presidency, it drew focus and funds from issues at home.

A former colony of France, Vietnam had been divided at the Geneva Accords in 1954. Anti-colonials led by Ho Chi Minh, who was also a communist, took the northern half of the country. The French colonial government took the southern part. The country was supposed to be reunited by elections in 1956, but the United States supported a government led by Ngo

Dinh Diem, a Vietnamese Catholic, in the south. It was understood that, in return for US support, Diem would distribute land to peasants and make other economic reforms. Communist China and the Soviet Union supported the Communist government led by Minh in the north.

Beginning in 1957, the northern communists, known as the Viet Minh (named after their leader, Ho Chi Minh) found people living in South Vietnam who were unhappy about the new Diem government. The northern communists began to supply these discontented South Vietnamese, called the Viet Cong, with supplies and weapons to conduct guerilla warfare against the Diem government. Guerilla warfare uses small groups of armed civilians in hit-and-run attacks and raids to fight a traditional military.

TROOPERS OF THE 327TH INFANTRY, 101ST AIR CAVALRY DIVISION, PATROL THE LAOTIAN BORDER, AUGUST 14, 1968

President Eisenhower famously explained the situation in Vietnam using his "domino theory" metaphor: If even one country in Southeast Asia were allowed to fall to communism, then eventually they all would. The United States was committed to aiding South Vietnam, sending about $2 billion and about 1,000 military advisors.

During the Kennedy administration, the United States increased military aid and advisors (up to about 16,000) to South Vietnam, hoping that it might eventually be able to defend itself. Instead, it became evident that the South Vietnamese Leader Diem was a problem. He had failed to make the land reforms that he had promised and was persecuting Buddhists by imprisoning or killing them and burning their temples. About three-quarters of Vietnam's population was Buddhist, though most of the Diem government was Catholic. Shortly before his own assassination, JFK approved a military coup to overthrow Diem in November 1963.

Diem was succeeded by several unstable military leaders, and the Viet Cong gained more influence over the South Vietnamese countryside. In August 1964, North Vietnamese boats attempted to torpedo the USS *Maddox*, a US ship on patrol in the Gulf of Tonkin, international waters off the coast of Vietnam. One week later, Congress passed the Tonkin Gulf Resolution. While not exactly a declaration of war, it authorized the president to take whatever military actions he felt were needed to promote security in Southeast Asia.

The United States launched Operation Rolling Thunder, its first sustained bombing attack of North Vietnam, in February 1965. By February 1966, the United States had sent around 200,000 ground troops to fight the Viet Cong. This policy of increasing engagement in a war is called escalation.

MATTER OF CHOICE: ESCALATING THE WAR IN VIETNAM

After the *Maddox* incident, military experts pushed for escalation. These pro-war "hawks" wanted the United States to employ massive aerial bombings and nuclear threats. Congressional "doves," on the other hand, hoped that President Johnson would use negotiations to get the country out of the war. Johnson feared the judgment of history—he neither wanted to "lose" Vietnam, nor did he want to be so involved in the conflict as to risk further Chinese involvement. He chose a middle-of-the-road approach that allowed some aerial bombing and sent more ground troops, but this ended up costing him his credibility with the American people.

In late 1967, William Westmoreland, the US military chief in Vietnam, made several optimistic statements regarding the progress of the war. Then in January 1968, the Viet Cong launched the Tet Offensive, a huge attack on 100 South Vietnamese towns and 12 air force bases. Though militarily the Tet Offensive was a loss for the Viet Cong, it was a psychological turning point for the American public. Many began to distrust the Pentagon's war reports and disapproved of the way LBJ handled the war. Anti-war protestors began taunting LBJ during his public appearances.

Meanwhile, the US inflation rate had tripled, and military spending was taking money away from Johnson's Great Society. Escalation had failed and cost LBJ the success of his cherished domestic programs. President Johnson announced that he would not run for reelection in 1968. The new president would have to figure out how to extricate the United States from Vietnam.

The Civil Rights Movement Continues

As the Vietnam War was being waged overseas, Black Americans and their allies were fighting another battle at home. After the success of the Montgomery bus boycott in 1956 and the formation of the Southern Christian Leadership Conference (SCLC), civil rights activists were eager to continue their fight for equality.

Ella Baker founded the Student Nonviolent Coordinating Committee (SNCC) in 1960. To protest the treatment of Black people at segregated restaurants and government offices, SNCC organized sit-ins, in which activists would simply enter a public place, such as a restaurant, and sit quietly as they were refused service. White onlookers would often taunt, insult, and throw food at the protesters, which was portrayed in news coverage. This display of how Black people were being treated got the activists' point across, and increased support for the movement.

Two Supreme Court decisions in 1946 and 1960 had made segregation illegal in interstate travel and the facilities associated with interstate travel. In May 1961, activists from the Congress of Racial Equality (CORE) planned what they called the Freedom Rides to test the court's decisions. The first set of freedom riders made it from Washington, DC, to Alabama, where they were met by mobs of racist white people who firebombed one of the buses. Fortunately, the riders escaped from the bus before it exploded. James Farmer, one of the leaders of CORE, called off the ride.

SNCC volunteers began a second Freedom Ride three days later, traveling from Nashville, Tennessee, to Birmingham, Alabama. The riders were arrested for breaking segregation laws and left stranded in Birmingham for several days. Attorney General Robert F. Kennedy arranged for state troopers to escort the riders to Montgomery, Alabama, where they were to be met by local police. When the riders arrived, the state troopers left, but the local police never showed up. Instead, a white mob attacked the undefended riders with bats and lead pipes.

When Martin Luther King Jr. heard of the violence, he organized a rally in support of the Freedom Rides at a local church, attracting another violent white mob. King called Attorney General Kennedy, who sent federal marshals to protect those inside the church and the riders. Soon after, President Kennedy directed the Interstate Commerce Commission to enforce the ban on segregation on all interstate buses and in associated facilities. The rides had been effective in attracting national attention and thereby putting pressure on the federal government to act.

After the Freedom Rides, school segregation issues resurfaced. In September 1962, James Meredith, a Black man, arrived on the campus of the all-white University of Mississippi to register for classes. Ross Barnett, the governor of Mississippi, had state troopers standing by to stop Meredith. Though President Kennedy ordered 120 federal marshals to escort Meredith upon his return to the school a few days later, a violent mob threw rocks and bottles at him. The marshals had to threaten to arrest Governor Barnett before he would allow Meredith to attend. Meredith became the first Black person to attend and graduate from the University of Mississippi.

In 1963, Martin Luther King Jr., along with the SCLC, joined a huge nonviolent campaign against segregation in Birmingham, Alabama. Hundreds of protestors were arrested, and the state court issued an order against the protests. MLK continued to protest and was jailed, but the SCLC had run out of bail money. Local officials would not allow King to call his wife, and so he remained in jail for eight days until the Kennedy administration intervened.

The protests continued, and local police used high-pressure fire hoses, clubs, and dogs to attack the peaceful protestors, some of whom were children. The images of such violence on TV and in the newspapers outraged Americans, so President Kennedy sent a representative to negotiate a truce between the activists and the city's leadership. On June 11, 1963, JFK proposed a new civil rights bill that would ban segregation in public facilities. However, Southern Democrats stalled the bill's progress in Congress.

To pressure the government to take action to ensure equality, 250,000 people participated in the March on Washington for Jobs and Freedom in August 1963, where MLK made his famous "I Have a Dream" speech. After Kennedy's assassination, President Johnson finally signed the Civil Rights Act of 1964 into law on July 2.

FOCUS POINT:
THE CIVIL RIGHTS ACT OF 1964

Though numerous court cases in the 1940s and 1950s struck down segregation as unconstitutional, it was still necessary for Congress to pass legislation to enforce integration in the South. The Civil Rights Act of 1964 officially prohibits "discrimination or segregation on the grounds of race, color, religion, or national origin," then goes on to specifically mention a long list of places to which the law applies, so that there could be no room for misinterpretation. It also includes clauses to establish a Civil Rights Commission to facilitate voter registration, integration in schools, and nondiscrimination in federal programs. This legislation went a long way toward ending segregation in the South.

In summer of 1964, called the "Freedom Summer," a group of about 1,000 volunteers organized by SNCC's Robert Moses arrived in Mississippi to register Black people to vote and to establish Freedom Schools. These schools were intended to prepare young Black people to continue with the civil rights movement once the summer volunteers were gone. The volunteers tried to register about 17,000 Black citizens, but local governments only accepted 1,600 of the applications. Additionally, members of the Ku Klux Klan, a white supremacist hate group, kidnapped and murdered three of the volunteers. The events of the Freedom Summer showed that further legislation was necessary to ensure that African Americans did not continue to be deprived of their right to vote.

To pressure Congress to pass such a law, the SCLC led a march from Selma, Alabama, to Montgomery, Alabama. Local police beat and gassed the marchers. In response, President Johnson introduced a bill that month to rid the South of literacy tests and poll taxes that were frequently used to prevent Black people from voting. Literacy tests had previously been a requirement for voting because it had been illegal to teach enslaved people to read, so most formerly enslaved people were illiterate. As time passed, white and Black Americans were given different literacy tests, with the questions on the Black literacy tests being almost impossible to answer—another example of institutional racism. The bill also allowed the federal government the right to assume authority over the registration of voters in areas where discrimination had been an issue. LBJ signed the bill, which became the Voting Rights Act of 1965, into law on August 6 of that year.

Black Power

By 1965, the civil rights movement had made some great strides in changing the laws that dictated how Black and white people interacted in the South. Segregation and voter repression had become illegal, and schools were on their way to being integrated. Unfortunately, this did not solve all the problems of discrimination that Black people (and other groups, whom we'll address in the next chapter) faced. It's one thing to change the law; it's quite another thing to change customs and attitudes.

Black people still faced social and economic inequality. In the North, even though there had been no official segregation, housing covenants forbade real estate agents and banks from allowing Black people to live in certain neighborhoods. As a result, Black Americans were relegated to small slums. In these areas, the only housing available was run by landlords who often didn't pay attention to health or housing regulations. Schools, public transportation, and employment opportunities in these areas were also dismal.

Police departments treated people of color unfairly, which led to violence in the mid-1960s. In 1964, a six-day riot broke out in Harlem, New York, after a white, off-duty police officer shot and killed a Black teenager. The next year, the arrest of two Black men for speeding in the Watts neighborhood of Los Angeles, California, set off a five-day riot. The National Guard was called to squelch it.

Another area of significant inequality was the Vietnam draft. In 1967, though Black young men made up 11% of the population, they represented 16% of those drafted for war. Forty percent of one special program to increase US troop presence in Vietnam (called Project 100,000) were Black draftees.

These continued injustices led to a rising sentiment that the nonviolent approach had only gone so far, and maybe it was time for a different strategy. Stokely Carmichael, a member of SNCC, began calling for Black Power, a movement encouraging Black people to be proud of their race and stop waiting on white people to "give" them equality. Proponents of Black Power argued that they should not have to blend in or act like white people to be treated with respect.

Another group, called the Black Panthers, was founded by Huey P. Newton and Bobby Seale. The Black Panthers wore military-looking clothing and openly carried guns as they patrolled their neighborhoods to defend inhabitants against police brutality. They wrote a 10-point manifesto that included demands for full employment, adequate housing, quality education, an end to police brutality, and fair treatment in the justice system. They provided much-needed social services in communities, including a free breakfast program for children that the government later adopted nationwide.

BLACK PANTHER PARTY MEMBERS IN OAKLAND, CALIFORNIA, 1968

As a result of the reports on the recent racial violence by the Kerner Commission, which had been established by President Johnson, Congress took up a new civil rights bill. Tragically, Martin Luther King Jr. was assassinated on April 4, 1968, leading to another huge wave of civil unrest. This motivated Congress to pass the bill quickly. President Johnson signed the Civil Rights Act of 1968 on April 11. The act allowed for the federal prosecution of hate crimes, prohibited some discrimination in housing rentals or sales (though it specifically allowed discrimination against those with disabilities and LGBTQ people), and included an "anti-riot act."

The civil rights movement's successes up to this point would inspire other groups—like women, Latinos, Indigenous peoples, Asian Americans, and LGBTQ people—to fight for their rights as well.

The Stonewall Rebellion and the LGBTQ Rights Movement

Before the 21st century, American culture as a whole was not friendly to LGBTQ people. Many people who identify as LGBTQ were discriminated against or treated with violence. In many places, it was illegal to participate in certain kinds of same-sex activities in public, such as holding hands or dancing. Homophobia, or a prejudice against gay people, was widespread.

In 1960s New York, due to certain anti-gay laws, gay bars were really the only places where LGBTQ people could socialize with one another openly. To get around police regulations and harassment, many of these bars were owned by the Mafia, who bribed local police. In exchange, police would warn these bar owners before they were raided so employees could hide unlicensed liquor.

On June 28, 1969, though, the police didn't tip off the Genovese crime family, who owned the Stonewall Inn in Greenwich Village in New York City. During their raid, the police arrested 13 people, handling them roughly as they were forced into the police vehicles. Onlookers began to throw nearby objects at the police, and soon a full-fledged riot had broken out. The police locked themselves inside the bar as the mob tried to set it on fire, but they were eventually rescued by the local fire department and police riot squad. Violent demonstrations reoccurred throughout the neighborhood for the next five days.

A GAY FREEDOM DAY PARADE IN SAN FRANCISCO, JUNE 1968

The Stonewall Rebellion inspired more activism. A gay power march led by a group called the Mattachine Society led to the formation of new groups, such as the Gay Liberation Front and the Gay Activist Alliance, and a special rally on the first anniversary of the riots. Craig Rodwell, an activist who owned the first gay bookstore in the country, organized what was then called the Christopher Street Liberation Day March. It became an annual event that eventually evolved into Gay Pride Day, which is now celebrated worldwide on the last Sunday in June. However, LGBTQ people faced a long struggle for equality and cultural acceptance that would span the rest of the 20th century.

CHAPTER 7

ROOTS OF MODERN CONSERVATISM

By the end of the 1960s, the United States had been on a liberal path for about 20 years. The administrations of Democratic presidents like Franklin D. Roosevelt and Lyndon B. Johnson enacted social reforms that made life better for many, but also increased the amount of control the government had over Americans' everyday lives. The counterculture movements of the 1950s and 1960s embraced nontraditional ways of living that seemed chaotic and threatening to conservative Americans. In the 1970s and 1980s, a sort of backlash occurred. The 1970s were characterized by a sense of malaise, or discomfort. This eventually led to the emergence of a strong conservative movement and, in the 1980s, culminated in the presidency of Ronald Reagan, whose administration embodied the economic and political ideals of traditional Republicans.

Women's Liberation Movement

While white women had gained some political equality with the passage of the Nineteenth Amendment in the 1920s, all women still suffered from social and economic inequalities throughout the first half of the 20th century. And like many groups in the 1960s, some women felt alienated and dissatisfied with society's expectations of them. Having witnessed the successes of the civil rights movement, they organized to promote their own interests.

It started with the publication of a book called *The Feminine Mystique* in 1963. Its author, Betty Friedan, wrote about "the problem that has no name," the feelings of boredom and alienation that came along with the 1950s ideal of suburban motherhood. Friedan argued that women should be free to pursue careers outside the home. But Friedan neglected to consider the probability that only white, middle- and upper-class women suffered from this problem. In the 1960s, about 40% of women worked outside the home.

Certain jobs, such as teacher, nurse, secretary, telephone operator, maid, and nanny, were considered "women's work." These roles paid far less than did men's jobs—even when the men did exactly the same work. Additionally, women in the workplace often endured what would be considered sexual harassment today. This included male co-workers criticizing their appearance or making unwanted romantic advances while management looked the other way.

Nonetheless, Friedan's book became popular among white, middle-class women, and it raised awareness of the inequality between the sexes. The Civil Rights Act of 1964, which forbade discrimination based on race, national origin, religion, or sex, provided a legal foundation for feminists—those who believed that women and men should be treated equally.

A MARCH FOR WOMEN'S LIBERATION IN NEW YORK CITY, 1971

The National Organization for Women (NOW) was founded in 1966 to "bring women into full participation in the mainstream of American society now, exercising all the privileges and responsibilities thereof in truly equal partnership with men." Some of the early reforms that NOW advocated for included equal access to education and job training, strict enforcement of the Civil Rights Act of 1964 with regard to employment discrimination, and government and employer support for childcare so mothers could work.

By the early 1970s, the movement could boast some successes. The Equal Employment Opportunity Commission had begun enforcing anti-discrimination laws, and women could now access a wide variety of jobs that had previously been unavailable to them. Parents could now deduct childcare expenses from their taxes. Title IX of the Higher Education

Act allowed women to attend any school, college, or university supported by federal funding and promoted the creation of women's sports teams.

Despite these gains, women were still not considered constitutionally equal to men. Though the Fourteenth Amendment guarantees all citizens equal protection under the law, it does not specifically mention women and has not been uniformly applied to sex discrimination cases. In 1972, the Equal Rights Amendment (ERA), which states that "equality of rights under the law shall not be denied or abridged by the United States or by any state on account of sex," was introduced. To be added to the Constitution, the amendment had to be approved by 38 states by 1982, but only 35 states had ratified it by the deadline. Phyllis Schlafly, a conservative activist who opposed the ERA, argued that its passage would make women eligible for the military draft. Others argued that the ERA would make it more difficult to pass legislation that specifically protected women. It appeared that the ERA had been defeated.

However, women's rights organizers have recently renewed their efforts to have the ERA ratified. They argue that there is no legal basis for putting a time limit on an amendment, and the House of Representatives voted in February 2020 to remove the limit. A resolution to lift the deadline has also been presented to the Senate. Three states have ratified the ERA since 2017. If the issues regarding the deadline can be resolved, the ERA might finally become part of the Constitution.

In 1973, the Supreme Court ruled that abortion is legal during the first three months of a woman's pregnancy, and states must not impose any restrictions on a woman's right to a legal abortion. After the second trimester, states may impose restrictions and prohibitions on the procedure to protect the fetus. This was a major victory for the women's rights movement, as it further allowed women to exert control over childbearing and freed them to pursue their educations or careers. However, many conservatives who were angered by the decision hope to have it overturned in the near future.

End of the Vietnam War: Peace but Not Honor

The civil war in Vietnam dragged on through three decades. The US policy of escalation had resulted in about 35,000 young men being drafted each month. At first, college students were exempt from the draft. In the 1960s, most college students were from affluent families, so a disproportionate number of draftees were from working-class and minority backgrounds.

Meanwhile, Americans were getting conflicting reports about how the war was going. Vietnam is often called the first "television war" due to the availability of film footage on news programs. Television reporter Walter Cronkite proclaimed after reporting on the Tet Offensive that the war was "mired in stalemate," meaning that no one was winning or losing. These images and reports contradicted White House press briefings, which had convinced Americans that the United States was close to winning. This resulted in a "credibility gap," an unwillingness to trust the government to tell the truth about what was really happening.

In the mid-1960s, the first baby boomers were becoming young adults, and the war seemed especially problematic to them due to the unfairness of the draft, seeming deception of the government, and inability of those under the age of 21 to vote. In the spring of 1968 alone, there were more than 200 major demonstrations against the war. Protesters burned draft cards, threw rocks and plastic bags full of urine at the police, and chanted, "Hey, hey, LBJ—how many kids did you kill today?"

President Johnson had declined to run for reelection in 1968 due to the public's dissatisfaction with US progress in the war. The new president, Richard Nixon, used a strategy he called "Vietnamization," the gradual withdrawal of US troops from Vietnam while training the South Vietnamese to defend themselves. This was supposed to allow the United States to have "peace with honor."

Yet in May 1969, Americans learned that the United States had begun secretly bombing Cambodia in March. (Cambodia is just to the west of South Vietnam, and the Viet Minh used the country as a base to supply weapons to the Viet Cong.) The next year, Nixon announced that US troops had invaded Cambodia, triggering another wave of protests. Members of the Ohio National Guard shot unarmed students—both protestors and passersby—at Kent State University, killing four students. Ten days later, police killed two students and injured 12 more at Jackson State University in Mississippi.

Finally, 19 years after Vietnam was divided at the 17th parallel, North and South Vietnam negotiated a ceasefire agreement in January 1973. American troops withdrew from the country two months later, and it seemed that containment had been achieved. However, by 1975, the North had invaded the South, captured the capital city of Saigon, and reunited all of Vietnam under one communist government. US intervention in Vietnam had failed, at the cost of more than 58,000 American lives and two million Vietnamese lives.

Nixon's Domestic Policies

Recreational drug use had increased during the 1960s, in large part due to the counterculture's embrace of altered states of consciousness. Additionally, in 1971, the military became aware that around 15% of enlisted men in Vietnam were using heroin, which was worrisome because of Nixon's Vietnamization strategy; it would be much tougher to deal with heroin addiction when troops returned home than it was to address the situation while they were still in Vietnam. As a result, Nixon announced his "War on Drugs" in June 1971. This included more funding for drug control agencies and the creation of the Drug Enforcement Agency (DEA).

Nixon, a Republican, was up for reelection in 1972 and sought the support of pro-segregation white voters in the South who had defected from the Democratic Party. Prior to 1948, most Southerners had been Democrats—a legacy of the Civil War. They remembered the radical Republicans who had forced Reconstruction upon them as villains, and so were staunchly loyal to the Democratic Party. Conversely, Black voters were often just as adamantly Republican, as it was "the party of Lincoln." This may seem a little backward to anyone familiar with today's politics—how did this come about?

Was the War on Drugs a success? It depends on whom you ask. The Richard Nixon Foundation claimed it was "incredibly successful," an evaluation backed up with some cherry-picked statistics. For instance, it found that as more people signed up for heroin treatment, crime rates fell in 72 cities. However, many other sources criticize the program for imprisoning thousands of people for nonviolent offenses and particularly for its systemic racism. The mandatory minimum sentencing associated with Nixon's "war" penalized crack users, who tended to be Black, much more heavily than it did powder cocaine users, who tended to be white. Other critics argue that criminalizing all sorts of drugs denies the government the chance to analyze and regulate them, thus making them even more dangerous.

Beginning with the 1932 election of Franklin D. Roosevelt, groups of people who had traditionally been Republicans began to switch their loyalties to the Democratic Party for different reasons, forming what is often called the "New Deal Coalition." Unemployed blue-collar workers and economically depressed Black people were attracted to Roosevelt's policies for creating jobs; Jews supported him due to his leadership against Nazi Germany. Then in 1948, the Democratic Party included a commitment to getting rid of "racial, religious, and economic discrimination," and in the early 1960s, Democrats John F. Kennedy and Lyndon B. Johnson supported civil rights. Pro-segregation Southerners had voted for independent candidates in the elections of 1948 and 1960, and were, in a sense, "up for grabs." In both the 1968 and 1972 elections, Nixon made it clear that he would be very conservative with regard to racial issues. Nixon's strategy worked. The Republican Party continues to be attractive to conservative white Southerners in modern elections.

All of Nixon's presidency was fairly eventful, but it is the end of his time in office that is most memorable. The security chief of the Committee to Re-Elect the President (CREEP) and four former CIA operatives were discovered breaking in to the Democratic National Committee headquarters. They had planned to photograph documents and check wiretapping equipment that they had previously installed. This was called the Watergate scandal, because the break-in occurred at the Watergate office complex.

At first, Nixon distanced himself from the break-in, but two newspaper reporters discovered that the incident was part of a group of illegal activities committed to destroy Nixon's political opposition. The burglars and their bosses were tried and convicted, and a White House aide told a Senate investigative committee that Nixon recorded all of his Oval Office conversations on audiotape. After Nixon refused to release the tapes to Congress despite a court order, the House Judiciary Committee began to investigate him to determine whether there were legal grounds for his impeachment. (This means that the House of Representatives has officially accused the president of a crime. For a president to be removed from office, the Senate must then hold an impeachment trial, and the president must be convicted by a two-thirds vote.)

After the Judiciary Committee passed three articles of impeachment and after being ordered by the Supreme Court to give up the tapes, Nixon was finally linked to the burglary. He resigned on August 8, 1974, before he could be officially impeached. Vice President Gerald Ford took office as president. About a month later, Ford publicly pardoned Nixon on television.

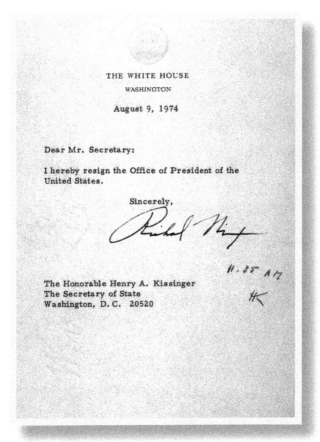

THE WHITE HOUSE
WASHINGTON

August 9, 1974

Dear Mr. Secretary:

I hereby resign the Office of President of the
United States.

Sincerely,

[signature: Richard Nixon]

11.35 AM

The Honorable Henry A. Kissinger
The Secretary of State
Washington, D.C. 20520

HK

NIXON'S RESIGNATION LETTER, SIGNED AUGUST 9, 1974

The scandal was important for several reasons. First, the Supreme Court defined executive privilege—what Nixon claimed to have that allowed him to withhold the tapes. The court determined that executive privilege is very limited and only applies to military or domestic affairs. Second, Watergate demolished what little trust Americans had for the government and led to long-lasting divisions between Republicans and Democrats that continue to plague Congress, making it difficult to pass legislation.

Gerald Ford, who became president after Nixon's resignation, officially pardoned Nixon on national television shortly after taking office in 1974. He explained that he wanted to prevent a trial or conviction from distracting the government from dealing with other political problems. Ford also referenced a Supreme Court case from 1915, in which the justices ruled that the acceptance of a pardon implies an admission of guilt.

A New Right

As the success of President Nixon's Southern strategy showed, there were large groups of people in the United States who supported conservative values. The civil rights movement, women's liberation, court decisions that prohibited required prayer and Bible reading in public schools, and the cultural values of hippies collectively alarmed some Americans, particularly evangelical Christians and corporate leaders. This group of people came together politically in the 1970s to form the "New Right." (Political ideology can be thought to exist on a spectrum. Conservatives are often referred to as "right-wing" and tend to be tradition-oriented and nationalist, while those on the left tend to focus on progress and equality.)

The rise of the New Right is often traced to the presidential candidacy of Barry Goldwater in 1964. Goldwater wanted the government to cut back its spending on social programs to lower taxes and eschew regulations on corporations and businesses that hindered economic growth. When Lyndon

B. Johnson won the 1964 election and put his Great Society program into effect, Goldwater's ideas began to appeal to a larger group. To them, Johnson's social programs seemed a lot like socialism.

The goals of the New Right included outlawing abortion, preventing the ratification of the Equal Rights Amendment, returning required prayer and religious activities to public schools, and freeing businesses of what they deemed to be excessive environmental and safety regulations. Many business leaders, white Southerners, northern blue-collar workers, Catholics, and evangelical Christians coalesced behind the New Right. The Moral Majority, a conservative political organization, was founded in 1979 by a Baptist televangelist named Jerry Falwell. Falwell's organization and other conservative groups raised money to ensure the defeat of liberal politicians. These groups contributed to the election of Ronald Reagan in 1980.

America in the Middle East

One factor contributing to the conservative backlash against liberalism was what President Jimmy Carter labeled a "crisis of confidence" during the 1970s. High unemployment, high inflation (meaning money doesn't go as far), and American dependence on oil from the Middle East contributed to this malaise.

The country's foreign relations problems with nations in the Middle East stemmed from the World War II era. The United States and Great Britain had supported the creation of the country of Israel as a homeland for Jews in 1948. This new Jewish state was established in Palestine, a territory north of the Arabian Peninsula, which both Jews and Palestinians claimed as a home. This created a conflict that continued throughout the 20th century and turned many Arab nations against the United States.

GAS STATION ATTENDANTS AT A PORTLAND, OREGON GAS STATION,
NOVEMBER 1973

In 1973, after Egyptian and Syrian forces attacked Israel in the hopes of regaining some lost territory, the United States sent emergency military aid to Israel. As a result of this interference, the Organization of the Petroleum Exporting Countries (OPEC) stopped oil shipments to the United States, causing a gasoline shortage. Even after the embargo was lifted in 1974, the now-quadrupled price of oil wreaked havoc on the US economy throughout the decade.

Further complicating the situation was US interference in Iran. In 1951, Operation Ajax and the overthrow of Prime Minister Mossadegh caused the United States to fall into serious disfavor with the Iranian people. The shah ruled Iran until 1979, when revolutionaries supported his overthrow in favor of a Muslim leader, Ayatollah Khomeini, who pledged to set up an Islamic Republic. The shah fled Iran, and later that year was allowed into the United States for cancer treatment.

The Khomeini government demanded the shah's return to Iran. When the United States declined, Iranian students took control of the US embassy in Tehran and held 52 Americans hostage for 444 days. This Iran Hostage Crisis further damaged the United States' already fragile relationship with Arab nations in the Middle East, leading to repercussions throughout the rest of the 20th century.

Reagan's Domestic Policies

President Carter's perceived mishandling of the Iran Hostage Crisis and growing discontent over the economic malaise of the 1970s combined with the influence of the New Right to get Republican President Ronald Reagan elected to the presidency in 1980. Because the Reagan administration turned away from the liberal "big government" programs of the past 40 years, his time in office is often referred to as the "Reagan Revolution."

Reagan instituted a package of new economic policies—called "Reaganomics," based on the theory of trickle-down economics. According to this economic philosophy, if the government helps those at the top of the economic hierarchy, such as corporations and wealthy taxpayers, then they will invest their extra money in ways that will help those lower down in the hierarchy. For example, if a business owner's taxes were decreased, then they would be able to hire more employees, thus creating jobs that would benefit more working-class people. In this way, money and prosperity is supposed to "trickle down" to everyone, even though the government policies officially benefit the richest. Reagan emphasized tax cuts, reduced government spending, and less government regulation to revive the economy.

To lower taxes, the Reagan administration radically changed the income tax code. The United States employs a graduated income tax, meaning that those who make more money each year are taxed at a higher percentage than are those who earn less. The Reagan administration reduced the highest individual tax rate by 42% and reduced corporate tax rates by 14%.

Of course, if the country is taking in less tax revenue (income), it will either have to spend less or borrow money. The Reagan administration cut government spending on social programs to reduce the federal budget by about 25%. Another way in which the government saved money was through deregulation, or removing or reducing government regulation of industry to foster greater competition among companies, which usually results in lower prices for consumers. During Reagan's presidency, occupational safety, consumer protection, banking, and transportation regulations were all significantly reduced.

Interestingly, the government *increased* military spending to 43% more than it had been during the height of the Vietnam War. This money was spent on a strategy called "Peace through Strength." The idea was that if the United States built up a huge arsenal of weapons to show its might, then it would intimidate the Soviet Union and prevent future clashes. The most famous aspect of this program was the Strategic Defense Initiative (SDI). Reagan imagined a system of satellites and lasers that were to be positioned in space to intercept Soviet missiles before they could strike the United States, and he called upon scientists to research and develop it. However, the necessary technology did not yet exist, so the SDI never materialized, even though the US spent a trillion dollars exploring the idea.

Reaganomics was only partially successful in achieving its goals. The tax cuts helped end the recession after 1981, and inflation slowed. However, because the government did not decrease its spending, the cuts to domestic social programs were canceled out by the spending on Peace through Strength. The government deficit—the difference between how much money the government brings in and how much it spends—increased from about 78 billion dollars to 152 billion dollars in just eight years. The deregulation of the banking industry directly contributed to the failure of about a third of the savings and loan associations during the late 1980s and early 1990s. (These institutions accept savings deposits and lend money for home mortgages and cars.)

Another domestic issue that the Reagan administration focused on was a renewal of Nixon's war on drugs. Around 1980, drug dealers had developed a new form of cocaine, called crack. They converted powdered cocaine into small pebbles that could be smoked, producing a more intense high. Because it was much cheaper than powdered cocaine, it was especially popular in poor, urban Black communities. In 1982, 4.2 million people reported regularly using cocaine; by 1985, the number had climbed to 5.8 million.

In response, the government began to make anti-drug policies that operated according to the theory of deterrence. The idea was that the threat of harsh punishment would prevent people from trying drugs in the first place. In 1986, the Anti-Drug Abuse Act established the practice of mandatory minimum sentencing for drug crimes. Possessing five grams of crack or 500 grams of powdered cocaine would result in five years in jail without parole. It also included a "three-strikes" provision that punished third-time drug offenders with life in prison without parole, no matter how minor or how long ago the previous offenses were. This provision took away judges' ability to consider all the factors in a case; the sentences were simply based on the type and weight of the drug involved.

Because Black people were more likely to use crack while white people were more likely to use powdered cocaine, many Black people caught with a small amount of crack were given longer sentences than white people caught with the same amount of powdered cocaine. As a result, a disproportionate number of Black people were incarcerated (put in jail).

President Reagan's wife, Nancy Reagan, started the "Just Say No" campaign to instill anti-drug attitudes in children. The campaign was widely criticized, because it didn't acknowledge that saying "no" isn't always so simple. Recent research shows that more successful drug programs help kids learn coping skills to deal with peer pressure and emphasize the detrimental health aspects of doing drugs.

CHAPTER 8

CHANGE AT HOME AND ABROAD

The 1980s and 1990s closed out the century with a long period of economic prosperity, fueled in part by the growth of technology. However, the country dealt with difficulties, including foreign policy issues related to the Middle East and domestic problems with illegal drug use, police brutality, and gun-related tragedies.

The First Personal Computer

It's tough to imagine life without computers, but they have really only been accessible to the masses since the 1970s. Though mechanical forerunners to the computer were developed as early as the 1830s, the first true computer did not come into use until 1943. Colossus I, a fully functioning electronic digital computer, was used at Bletchley Park, the British "intelligence factory," which housed codebreakers during World War II.

The first fully functioning electronic digital computer built in the United States was called ENIAC. It was developed in 1945 at the University of Pennsylvania. It was larger and more flexible than the Colossus, but like its predecessor, it served one primary function: calculating artillery trajectories.

ENIAC COMPUTER PARTS, 1946

It had no stored programs and had to be physically reset before each new job. Six years later, UNIVAC was completed. UNIVAC was the first general-purpose digital computer that could store programs. It was put into use by the US Census Bureau. These early computers were gigantic in comparison to what we are used to. Because of their size and cost, they were only used in government offices or by huge corporations.

By 1971, Intel had developed the first microprocessing chip, and IBM engineers produced the floppy disk, for information storage. Starting in 1974, minicomputers were available for sale to the general public. Soon after, Microsoft and Apple were founded, and programmers developed a word processor and spreadsheet program. In 1981, IBM introduced the first personal computer, called Acorn. It had an Intel microprocessor, two floppy disk drives, and a color monitor. Personal computer ownership grew rapidly in the 1980s and 1990s, laying the foundation for the Information Revolution and the Internet Age.

The Advent of the Internet

If it's difficult to imagine life without computers, it's probably even tougher to imagine life without the internet. You might imagine that it would feel like forgetting your cell phone and being "disconnected" from other people and quick access to information. Amazingly enough, it only took about 30 years for the internet to pervade our society. This is a fairly short amount of time for a cultural revolution; the Industrial Revolution, for example, took 150 years!

The internet's predecessor, called ARPANET, was developed in 1969 for use by the US Department of Defense to exchange information. Various protocols for communication among computers were used for the next decade or so, but only by the government and computer scientists. The internet's official birthday is January 1, 1983—when a new universal language was developed that allowed different networks of computers to connect (called TCP/IP). A few years later, Tim Berners-Lee invented the World Wide Web, and the first Web server in the United States came online in 1991. At first, the Web was not very user-friendly, but in 1993 several browsers were released to work with personal computers. In 1994, the media began to inform the public about the Web, and a search engine, Yahoo!, was developed.

The economy was doing well in the mid-1990s, and stock market investors had plenty of capital. A plethora of new internet and tech companies were created, and investors were eager to invest money in them, leading to stock market speculation, the practice of buying something when it is cheap, holding on to it until the value increases, and then selling it for a profit. One type of speculation that you might be familiar with is flipping houses. A person buys a "distressed" house, fixes it up, then sells it for way more than it originally cost.

During what is often called the "dot-com bubble," investors bought cheap stock in technology startup companies, hoping that when the companies began making a profit, the value of the stock would rise. Then they could resell the stock to make a profit, or keep the stock and earn dividends from the company. From 1995 to 2000, technology stock speculation resulted in a bull market—meaning the stock market is doing well. However, in 2000, the "bubble" burst, and many of the stocks dropped in value. This is called a bear market. The stock market crashed in 2002. This happened because many of the companies in which the investors had bought stock could not stay in business.

Of course, we know that this burst bubble wasn't the end of the internet. Companies like Amazon, Google, Microsoft, and Apple survived. Over the course of about 10 years, the internet completely changed many aspects of people's everyday lives. In the early '90s, if you wanted to call someone, you'd have to use a land line, and calling people outside of your own area code cost extra. To watch a TV show, you had to wait until it came on at its scheduled time. People had to rent or buy movies on VHS tapes and purchase radios, cassette tapes, or CDs to listen to music. Shopping malls were very popular, because that's where people went to buy things. Paper shopping catalogs allowed people to order consumer goods by mail.

In many ways, the internet has changed the world for the better, making it easier and faster to send or receive information, shop for practically anything from virtually anywhere, and access a world of entertainment on demand. We don't have to carry around or store physical media, and we can use less paper.

In other ways, though, the internet has caused problems. Psychologists argue that we are physically addicted to our phones and getting likes on social media. Others bemoan the lack of actual social connections due to technology. Additionally, if for some reason the internet goes down for a long period of time, many of us are lost. It's difficult to look up a phone number, use a map, or determine when a movie is going to start the "old-fashioned" way, because phone books, paper maps, and physical newspapers aren't as common.

Unfortunately, the resources accessible through the internet are not available to everyone: Lower-income households may not be able to afford internet service, laptops, and tablets. This is especially problematic in the education field, as schools rely on computers and the internet.

The Persian Gulf War

During the 1970s, the United States' dependence on oil from the Middle East became clear during the OPEC oil embargo of 1973, which caused fuel shortages and impacted the US economy for the rest of the decade. The embargo was triggered by

US support for Israel in the Yom Kippur War. Discord with the Middle East increased when the United States allowed the deposed shah of Iran to enter the country for cancer treatment, triggering the Iran Hostage Crisis. In the 1980s and 1990s, the need for easy access to Middle Eastern oil led to more US involvement in the Arabian Peninsula.

In 1990, Saddam Hussein, the dictator of Iraq, accused the nation of Kuwait of secretly stealing oil from oil fields on the two countries' shared border. He began to make financial demands of Kuwait and readied Iraqi troops along the Iraq–Kuwait border. Hussein ordered his troops to invade Kuwait on August 2, 1990.

Kuwait and its ally, Saudi Arabia, requested the United States' and NATO's help. The UN Security Council demanded that Iraq withdraw. Hussein ignored the ultimatum, instead formally annexing Kuwait (making it officially part of Iraq). The king of Saudi Arabia requested US assistance on August 6, and a US-led coalition of troops launched an air offensive on Iraq on January 17, 1991, known as Operation Desert Storm. The Iraqi air force was quickly destroyed. Kuwait was liberated, and President George H. W. Bush called a ceasefire on February 28. Hussein accepted peace terms requiring Iraq to recognize Kuwait as a sovereign (standalone) nation and eliminate Iraq's stockpile of nuclear, biological, and chemical weapons. That would require Iraq to allow UN weapons inspectors access to its weapons facilities.

Throughout the 1990s, Hussein refused to cooperate with the weapons inspectors, in violation of the terms of the ceasefire. This eventually led to another Iraqi war, often called Operation Iraqi Freedom, which began in 2003. This war focused on disarming Iraq (which turned out *not* to be manufacturing "weapons of mass destruction," as US politicians had claimed) and ousting Hussein. Though Hussein was captured in 2003 and executed in 2006, US troops remained in Iraq until 2011.

In 1994, the North American Free Trade Agreement (NAFTA) went into effect. This was a controversial agreement between Canada, the United States, and Mexico that removed most tariffs (taxes on imports) on goods produced in the three countries. It also made it easier for each country to pursue investments in the other countries. Supporters of NAFTA pointed out that it lowered the prices of many goods, boosted the US gross domestic product (GDP), and promoted diplomacy with Mexico. Critics argued that it led to the loss of American jobs, as many companies were able to operate more cheaply in Mexico by paying their workers lower wages.

The End of the Cold War

In 1985, the Soviet Union got a new premier (leader), Mikhail Gorbachev. He believed that the country needed some serious reform, because it was going bankrupt trying to keep up in the arms race against the United States. He instituted two new policies: glasnost (political openness) and perestroika (economic restructuring), and he worked to establish a friendlier relationship with the United States. He met with President Reagan twice to discuss a reduction in armaments for both countries. Within the Soviet satellite nations, rebellious groups gained power. When such a group rebelled in Poland in 1989, Gorbachev did not send Soviet troops to squelch the rebellion. Similar insurrections soon followed in Hungary, East Germany, Bulgaria, Czechoslovakia, and Romania. On

December 25, 1991, the Soviet Union simply ceased to exist, and the Cold War ended.

With no Soviet Union or satellite nations to defend against, the need to continue NATO was questioned. In response, British Prime Minister Margaret Thatcher remarked, "You don't cancel your home insurance policy just because there have been fewer burglaries on your street in the last 12 months!"

NATO took on a sort of "big brother" role, assisting countries that needed help with human rights crises and promoting the development of democracy in the nations that had been created by the Soviet Union's collapse. For example, NATO intervened in the Yugoslav Wars that occurred after the breakup of Yugoslavia (another communist state that dissolved in the early 1990s) and in Desert Storm. This quote from the NATO website summarizes its new purpose very nicely: "With the collapse of the Soviet Union and the rise of non-state actors affecting international security, many new security threats emerged. NATO is countering these threats by utilizing collective defense, managing crisis situations, and encouraging cooperative security . . ." The non-state actors it refers to are terrorist organizations—which became the main threat to US security around the turn of the 21st century.

In the mid-1980s, Soviet Premier Gorbachev began reforms that would eventually lead to the fall of the Soviet Union on December 25, 1991. With the Cold War seemingly nearing its end, the US government faced a decision regarding continuing the expensive arms race that had been a feature of the Reagan administration. President Reagan proposed the Strategic Arms Reduction Treaty (START), which George H. W. Bush and Gorbachev signed in 1991. The treaty limited the number of nuclear warheads and intercontinental ballistic missiles that each country could possess and was an important symbol of reconciliation at the end of the Cold War.

The LA Riots

Though the civil rights movement of the 1960s brought some relief from legal discrimination against Black Americans, plus women, religious minorities, and low-income families of all races, at the end of the 20th century, they still faced societal and cultural oppression. These tensions came into the limelight in 1991 with the police beating of Rodney King, a Black man from California.

Racial tensions were already high in South Los Angeles, which had a majority population of Black residents, a high unemployment rate, and problems with gang crime. Black residents of the area reported that local police were cruel and unfair to them. A month earlier, a teenage Black girl had been shot and killed by a Korean store owner, purportedly for stealing orange juice. Later, it was found that the girl had actually been holding the money to pay for the juice when she was killed. The store owner was sentenced to time served, 400 hours of community service, a $500 fine, and five years of probation.

On March 3, 1991, King was speeding on a Los Angeles freeway when the California Highway Patrol tried to pull him over. He resisted because he was on probation for robbery and had been drinking. After a high-speed chase, King eventually stopped in front of an apartment building. Four white police officers beat him with batons and kicked him for about 15 minutes, while more police officers watched. As a result of the beating, King suffered skull fractures, broken bones, and permanent brain damage.

Unbeknownst to the officers, a local man had filmed the beating from his apartment window, and he released the tape to a local TV station. The video went "viral," and people all over the country were outraged at the police officers' behavior. The officers were put on trial for excessive force, but a jury found them not guilty on April 29, 1992.

PEOPLE WALK BY A BURNED BUILDING IN SOUTH LOS ANGELES, 1992

When the verdict was announced, Angelenos reacted violently, setting things on fire and breaking into stores and stealing merchandise. For several hours after the riots started, the LA police stood by, unresponsive. It was not until the mayor of Los Angeles called the governor for help that National Guard troops showed up to end the rioting. After five days of unrest, more than 50 people were killed and more than 2,000 were injured. The majority were Black and Hispanic individuals. Almost 6,000 were arrested.

Martin Luther King Jr. once said, "A riot is the language of the unheard." The riots represented a voicing of a century of pent-up frustration at the problematic racial situations that still existed. These issues are still affecting the United States today. In recent years, racially motivated police brutality incidents, such as the killings of Trayvon Martin, Breonna Taylor, and George Floyd, have given birth to the Black Lives Matter social and political movement and created new national dialogues about systemic racism in the United States.

Gun Control

Gun control has been an issue in American politics since 1789, when the Bill of Rights included the Second Amendment, which reads, "A well-regulated militia, being necessary to the security of a free state, the right of the people to keep and bear arms shall not be infringed."

For more than two centuries, questions about the interpretation of the Second Amendment have arisen for many reasons. Concern over the regulation of firearms became more widespread after the assassinations of John F. Kennedy and Martin Luther King Jr. in the 1960s and the attempted assassination of Ronald Reagan in 1981. As President Reagan was leaving a Washington hotel in a limousine, a mentally unstable man, John Hinckley Jr., shot at the limousine, believing that it would impress actress Jodie Foster. He injured President Reagan, a secret service agent, a police officer, and White House Press Secretary James Brady. All the men survived, but Secretary Brady was permanently disabled and brain damaged.

Brady, his wife, and Reagan became gun control activists and vocally supported the Brady Bill, which would require anyone in the United States who wanted to purchase a firearm to have a background check and comply with a five-day waiting period. President Bill Clinton signed the bill into law in 1993, creating the Brady Handgun Violence Prevention Act. A year later, the Federal Assault Weapons Ban was passed, banning semi-automatic weapons and types of ammunition that held large numbers of bullets, or rounds.

Despite these new regulations, frightening instances of violence caused Americans to continue the debate over gun rights. In the late '90s, three instances of domestic terrorism took place that demonstrated the ability of motivated individuals to assemble or acquire weapons, even with the new restrictions. The Oklahoma City bombing, the capture of the Unabomber, and the massacre at Columbine High School served as examples of the havoc that individuals with easy access to firearms and explosives could wreak.

The Oklahoma City bombing occurred in April 1995, when a rental truck exploded in front of the Alfred P. Murrah Federal Building in Oklahoma City. The explosion killed 168 people, injured 650 others, and destroyed the entire north wall of the building, along with damaging or destroying 300 other nearby buildings. The explosion was found to have been caused by a homemade bomb created by Timothy McVeigh and Terry Nichols, members of a radical anti-government group. McVeigh was sentenced to the death penalty and executed in 2001; Nichols was sentenced to 161 consecutive life terms in prison.

OKLAHOMA CITY FIREFIGHTERS REMOVE RUBBLE FROM THE EXPLOSION SITE OF THE ALFRED P. MURRAH FEDERAL BUILDING, APRIL 1995

The Unabomber was an American domestic terrorist who had been mailing bombs, usually to university professors or computer stores, since 1978. By 1995, the FBI attributed 16 homemade explosives to the Unabomber. Then in June 1995, several prominent newspapers received an essay from the bomber, in which he criticized industrialization and technology. A woman named Linda Patrik read the essay and thought it sounded like the letters her brother-in-law sent to her husband. This led the FBI to the primitive forest cabin where Ted Kaczynski was found with the original copy of the essay and bomb-making supplies in April 1996. Kaczynski pled guilty to the bombings and was sentenced to four life terms in prison.

On April 20, 1999 at Columbine High School, located in a suburb of Denver, Colorado, two students shot and killed 13 people and wounded 20 others. The shooters had originally planned to bomb the school, having been inspired by the Oklahoma City bombing. They placed two homemade bombs in the cafeteria and went outside to their cars to watch the explosion, but the bombs did not detonate as planned. They reentered the school and shot students outside the entrance and in the hallways, cafeteria, and library. Police on the scene exchanged fire with the shooters several times but were unsuccessful at stopping the massacre. About 45 minutes after entering the school, the two shooters died by suicide in the library.

Investigations after the event showed that both boys had been planning the attack for about a year, and their diaries revealed signs of mental illness and bullying. The Columbine High School massacre was the deadliest school shooting in history at that time, and it led to increased school security measures, "zero-tolerance" discipline systems in schools, anti-bullying campaigns, and more concern regarding students' mental health. Despite that, more school shootings have occurred since Columbine, including those at Virginia Tech in 2007, Sandy Hook Elementary School in 2012, and Marjory Stoneman Douglas High School in 2018. Activists called for more gun-control measures, and some new legislation was passed to prevent adults from buying guns for minors; however, loopholes remain that make it possible to buy a gun without a background check in some situations.

According to the Fourth Amendment, people in the United States are free from unreasonable search and seizure—which means that law enforcement cannot search people or their possessions without a warrant or probable cause. TLO was a high school student whose purse was searched by a school administrator because she was found to be smoking cigarettes in a school restroom. The administrator found evidence in her purse of marijuana possession and distribution, as well as cigarettes. TLO sued for violation of her Fourth Amendment rights, but the Supreme Court ruled in 1985 that while in school, juveniles may be searched without a warrant or probable cause because school authorities have a need to maintain an educational environment at school. The moral of the story: The rights outlined in the Bill of Rights sometimes come with caveats, or limits.

LEGACY

T he 20th century represented a period of great change in the United States. Consider the position of the country at the beginning of the century. It had just won the Spanish-American War, its first defeat of a major European power. It was beginning to assert itself internationally but did not have much influence among the other European powers, which controlled huge global empires. Rapid industrialization after the Civil War gave the country economic dominance, but it was beset with nativism, racism, sexism, and bigotry. Over the course of the century, with respect to each of these issues, the United States underwent significant transformation.

Participation in the two world wars made the United States a major world power. US entry in both wars provided the Allies with fresh sources of troops, weapons, and cash, allowing the defeat of first the Central and then the Axis powers. In the aftermaths of both wars, US financial resources allowed war-damaged countries to recover and influenced the spread of democracy and capitalism in Europe and elsewhere, and they ensured that countries that received aid from the United States would be politically friendly in the future. In this way, the country gained power militarily, economically, and diplomatically.

The American economy changed from being oriented around industry and agriculture at the turn of the 20th century to being centered around service and information at the turn of the 21st century. The economy experienced several periods of difficulty that resulted in changing levels of government involvement. First, the Great Depression in the 1930s resulted in increased government regulation with the New Deal. Later, the economic malaise of the 1970s resulted in deregulation during the Reagan Era. The introduction of computers, the resulting information revolution, and trade agreements such as NAFTA changed the type of work available to Americans by making some jobs obsolete while shifting others overseas. Workers gained some protections through the work of labor unions, such as safer working conditions, the abolition of child labor, and limits on working hours. However, modern workers still deal with some unresolved issues, such as low wages, lack of good jobs for people of all education levels, and lack of health and retirement benefits.

With regard to issues of equality—nativism, racism, and sexism—once again, there has been significant change, but there is still room for improvement. The civil rights movement of the 1960s inspired other social justice movements, such as the women's liberation movement, American Indian movement, Chicano movement, Asian American movement, and LGBTQ movement, gaining different groups increased legal protections, reducing discrimination, and increasing acceptance of those groups in society. However, the United States has yet to achieve true equality of opportunity for all people.

Maybe the best way to think about the 20th century is to think of it as the rough draft of an essay. The United States had some great ideas and wrote several excellent sentences, but it still needs to do quite a bit of revising. Maybe with a few insertions and deletions, some rewording, and the consultation of a couple of fresh resources, the 21st century can turn out to be a really well-written final draft!

RESOURCES

BOOKS

A Different Mirror for Young People by Ronald Takaki and Rebecca Stefoff
A Different Mirror looks at US history from the viewpoint of different ethnic groups, using information from diaries, letters, and poems to capture the true experiences of people from the past.

A Young People's History of the United States by Howard Zinn and Rebecca Stefoff
Howard Zinn wrote the history of the United States from the point of view of "ordinary people," which makes it far more interesting and tells a very different story than what we usually learn in school.

American History: A Visual Encyclopedia by DK Children's Publishing and the Smithsonian Institution
This big, beautiful, colorful book has plenty of entries, with short, interesting readings to go along with each one.

The Reader's Companion to American History edited by Eric Foner and John Garraty
This book has both short blurbs, which give overviews on topics, and longer pieces, which provide the reader with a deeper understanding of more complicated issues when necessary. As a teacher, this is my go-to reference book when I need a quick refresher on a topic.

WEBSITES

American Experience
PBS.org/wgbh/americanexperience
Technically, *American Experience* is a documentary series on
PBS, but this website offers so much more. There are links to
full-length documentaries, short videos, and articles on just
about any topic you can think of throughout US history. I show
one *American Experience* documentary for every unit of my
US History class; students especially like the "Triangle Fire"
episode.

American Yawp
AmericanYawp.com
What the heck's a yawp? It's a raucous noise, of course! This
title refers to a line from a Walt Whitman poem: "I sound my
barbaric yawp over the roofs of the world." AmericanYawp
.com is an online collaborative text written by college history
professors, so it's in an academic tone. It's also *free*, so the
authors weren't constrained by some corporation or profit
motives to write about certain topics. As a result, it includes
some really unusual discussions of aspects of history that are
not frequently addressed in high school classrooms.

Black Past
BlackPast.org
This site focuses on both African American and African history. It is very accurate and visually stunning, with lots of great
pictures.

Crash Course US History with John Green
PBSLearningMedia.org/collection/crash-course-us-history
A series of short videos (usually lasting from eight to
12 minutes) covering topics in US history in a very humorous
yet accurate way. John Green actually cowrote the videos with
his high school history teacher!

National Women's History Museum

WomensHistory.org

This excellent online museum has lots of exhibits, document archives, articles, and my favorite: copious amounts of pictures!

Zinn Education Project

ZinnEdProject.org

This site includes articles based on the "people's history" approach that characterizes Howard Zinn's great book, *A People's History of the United States*.

SELECTED REFERENCES

Alice Paul Institute. "Why We Need the Equal Rights Amendment." 2018. EqualRightsAmendment.org/why.

American Heritage. "The Age of Steel." *American Heritage* 52, no. 4 (June 2001). AmericanHeritage.com/age-steel#2.

Augustyn, Adam. "Columbine High School Shootings." Britannica.com. Accessed October 28, 2020. Britannica .com/event/Columbine-High-School-shootings.

Chase, Alston. "Harvard and the Making of the Unabomber." *Atlantic* (June 2000). TheAtlantic.com/magazine /archive/2000/06/harvard-and-the-making-of-the -unabomber/378239.

Collins, Gail. "The Feminine Mystique at Fifty." *New York Times Magazine*, January 23, 2013. NYTimes.com /2013/01/27/magazine/the-feminine-mystique-at -50.html.

Danzer, Gerald A., et al. *The Americans: Reconstruction to the 21st Century*. Evanston, IL: McDougal Littell, 2006.

Elliott, Debbie. "Integrating Ole Miss: A Transformative, Deadly Riot." *Morning Edition*, National Public Radio, October 1, 2012. NPR.org/2012/10/01/161573289 /integrating-ole-miss-a-transformative-deadly-riot.

Federal Deposit Insurance Corporation. "The FDIC: A History of Confidence and Stability." Accessed September 19, 2020. FDIC.gov/exhibit/p1.html#/0.

Fetters, Ashley. "4 Big Problems with *The Feminine Mystique*." *Atlantic*, February 12, 2013. TheAtlantic.com/sexes /archive/2013/02/4-big-problems-with-the-feminine -mystique/273069.

Foner, Eric, and John A. Garraty, eds. *The Reader's Companion to American History*. Boston: Houghton Mifflin Company, 1991.

Franke-Ruta, Garance. "An Amazing 1969 Account of the Stonewall Uprising." *Atlantic*, January 24, 2013. TheAtlantic.com/politics/archive/2013/01/an-amazing -1969-account-of-the-stonewall-uprising/272467.

Fresh Air. "Great Migration: The African-American Exodus North." NPR.org, September 13, 2010. NPR.org/templates /story/story.php?storyid=129827444.

Grossmann, Jonathan. "The Coal Strike of 1902: A Turning Point in US Policy." US Department of Labor's *Monthly Labor Review* (June 1974). DOL.gov/general/aboutdol /history/coalstrike.

History.com Editors. "War on Drugs." History.com. Last modified December 17, 2019. History.com/topics/crime /the-war-on-drugs.

Holmes, Marian Smith. "Spies Who Spilled Atomic Bomb Secrets." *Smithsonian Magazine*, April 19, 2009. SmithsonianMag.com/history/spies-who-spilled -atomic-bomb-secrets-127922660.

Hymowitz, Carol, and Michaele Weissman. *A History of Women in America*. New York: Bantam Books, 1984.

Library of Congress. "Immigration to the United States, 1851–1900." LOC.gov. Accessed August 2020. LOC.gov /teachers/classroommaterials/presentationsand activities/presentations/timeline/riseind/chinimms /chinimms.html.

Library of Congress. "The Lusitania Disaster." LOC.gov. Accessed September 4, 2020. LOC.gov/collections /world-war-i-rotogravures/articles-and-essays /the-lusitania-disaster.

Locke, Joseph L., and Ben Wright, eds. *The American Yawp: A Massively Collaborative Open U.S. History Textbook, Vol. 1: To 1877.* Stanford, CA: Stanford University Press, 2019.

Maues, Julia. "Banking Act of 1933 (Glass-Steagall)." FederalReserveHistory.org. November 22, 2013. FederalReserveHistory.org/essays/glass-steagall-act.

McGrath, Michael. "Nancy Reagan and the Negative Impact of the 'Just Say No' Anti-Drug Campaign." *Guardian*, March 8, 2016. TheGuardian.com/society/2016/mar /08/nancy-reagan-drugs-just-say-no-dare-program -opioid-epidemic.

Michaels, Debra, ed. "Alice Paul." National Women's History Museum. 2015. WomensHistory.org/education -resources/biographies/alice-paul.

Moore, Cara. "Women Workers in Wartime." U.S. National Archives and Records Administration's *Prologue Magazine* 48, no. 3 (Fall 2016). Archives.gov/publications /prologue/2016/fall/women-workers.

Natanson, Barbara Orbach. "National Child Labor Committee Collection." LOC.gov. Accessed August 20, 2020. LOC.gov /pictures/collection/nclc/background.html.

National Association for the Advancement of Colored People. "NAACP Legal History." NAACP.org. Accessed August 20, 2020. NAACP.org/naacp-legal-team/naacp-legal-history.

National Constitution Center. "The Nixon Pardon in Constitutional Retrospect." *Constitution Daily*, September 8, 2020. ConstitutionCenter.org/blog/the-nixon-pardon-in-retrospect.

North Atlantic Treaty Organization. "A Short History of NATO." Accessed October 27, 2020. NATO.int/cps/en/natohq/declassified_139339.htm.

Ortiz, Paul. *An African-American and Latinx History of the United States*. Boston: Beacon Press, 2018.

Oyez.org. "Plessy v. Ferguson." Accessed August 2020. Oyez.org/cases/1850-1900/163us537.

Oyez.org. "Roe v. Wade." Accessed October 25, 2020. Oyez.org/cases/1971/70-18.

Pruitt, Sarah. "Why It Took 17 Years to Catch the Unabomber." History.com. October 25, 2018. History.com/news/unabomber-letter-bombs-investigation-arrest.

Records of the U.S. House of Representatives. Lend Lease Bill HR 77A-D13, Record Group 233, National Archives. 1941. OurDocuments.gov/doc.php?flash=false&doc=71.

Runtagh, Jordan. "Elvis Presley on TV: 10 Unforgettable Broadcasts." *Rolling Stone*, January 28, 2016. RollingStone.com/music/music-news/elvis-presley-on-tv-10-unforgettable-broadcasts-225225.

Sage, Henry J. "The War between Capital and Labor." SageAmericanHistory.net. Last updated February 5, 2018. SageAmericanHistory.net/gildedage/topics/capital_labor_immigration.html.

Sastri, Amjuli, and Karen Grigsby Bates. "When LA Erupted in Anger: A Look Back at the Rodney King Riots." NPR. April 16, 2017. NPR.org/2017/04/26/524744989 /when-la-erupted-in-anger-a-look-back-at-the -rodney-king-riots.

Shuster, Alvin M. "G.I. Heroin Addiction Epidemic in Vietnam." *New York Times*, May 16, 1971. NYTimes. com/1971/05/16/archives/gi-heroin-addiction -epidemic-in-vietnam-gi-heroin-addiction-is.html.

Siegel, Robert. "Jacob Riis: Shedding Light on NYC's 'Other Half.'" NPR's *All Things Considered*. June 30, 2008. NPR.org/templates/story/story.php?storyId=91981589.

Smith, Noah. "The 1950s Are Greatly Overrated." Bloomberg .com. November 1, 2019. Bloomberg.com/opinion /articles/2019-11-01/economic-growth-in-the-1950s -left-a-lot-of-americans-behind.

Smithsonian National Museum of American History. "White Only: Jim Crow in America." Accessed August 20, 2020. AmericanHistory.SI.edu/brown/history /1-segregated/white-only-1.html.

Stearns, Peter N., Michael B. Adas, Stuart B. Schwartz, and Marc Jason Gilbert. *World Civilizations: The Global Experience, Since 1200* (AP edition). 8th ed. London: Pearson, 2020.

Swaine, Michael R. "Computer." *Encyclopaedia Britannica*. Last updated August 13, 2020. Britannica.com /technology/computer.

Swoboda, Frank. "The Legacy of Deregulation." *Washington Post*, October 2, 1988. WashingtonPost.com/archive /business/1988/10/02/the-legacy-of-deregulation /c553674b-8bd2-436e-9be7-7de95f798fbb.

Takaki, Ronald. *A Different Mirror: A History of Multicultural America*. New York: Little, Brown & Company, 1993.

Tassava, Christopher. "The American Economy During World War II." EH.net Encyclopedia. February 10, 2008. EH.net /encyclopedia/the-american-economy-during-world -war-ii.

Thompson, Derek. "America in 1915: Long Hours, Crowded Houses, Death by Trolley." *Atlantic*, February 11, 2016. TheAtlantic.com/business/archive/2016/02/america -in-1915/462360.

Tindall, George Brown, and David Shi. *America: A Narrative History*. 8th ed. New York: W.W. Norton & Company, 2010.

Troy, Gil. "The Age of Reagan." Gilder Lehrman Institute of American History. Accessed October 15, 2020. AP.GilderLehrman.org/history-by-era/essays/age -reagan.

Turner, Deonna S. "Crack Epidemic." *Encyclopaedia Britannica*. Last updated September 4, 2017. Britannica .com/topic/crack-epidemic.

US National Archives and Records Administration. "Vietnam War U.S. Military Fatal Casualty Statistics." Archives.gov. Last updated April 30, 2019. Archives.gov/ research/military/vietnam-war/casualty-statistics.

———. "Women in the Work Force during World War II." Archives.gov. Last reviewed August 15, 2016. Archives. gov/education/lessons/wwii-women.html.

United States Senate. "The Censure Case of Joseph McCarthy of Wisconsin." Senate.gov. Accessed October 1, 2020. Senate.gov/about/powers-procedures/censure /133Joseph_McCarthy.htm.

University of California. "Everyday Life and People." 2009. Calisphere.org/exhibitions/27/everyday-life-and-people -in-the-early-20th-century.

University of Minnesota Libraries. 2016. "Understanding Media and Culture: The Relationship between Television and Culture." Open.Lib.UMN.edu/mediaandculture /chapter/9-2-the-relationship-between-television -and-culture.

US Securities and Exchange Commission. "What We Do." Last modified December 18, 2020. SEC.gov/about/what-we -do#create.

INDEX

Page numbers in *italics* indicate photographs

A

Aldrin, Buzz, 67

Alliance system, 27

American Federation of
    Labor, 21, 22

Anti-Drug Abuse Act (1986), 120

Appeasement, 44–45

Arms race, 27

Armstrong, Neil, 67

Atomic bombs, 47–48

B

Baby boom, 72–75

Baer, Elizabeth, 30

Baker, Ella, 95

Baker, Josephine, *35*

Barnett, Ross, 96

Beats, 84

Berlin, Battle of, 46

Berlin Blockade, 62

Berners-Lee, Tim, 126

Berry, Chuck, 77

Birth Control Clinical Research
    Bureau, 34

Black codes, 5

Black Lives Matter movement, 133

Black Panthers, 100

Black Power, 98–101

Brady, James, 134

Brady Bill, 134

Brady Handgun Violence
    Prevention Act (1993), 134

Brown v. Board of Education, 6, 78

Brown v. Board of Education II, 78

Bryan, William Jennings, 14

Buffalo Soldiers, 53

Bush, George H. W., 128, 131

C

Cambodia, 110

Capitalism, 70–72

Car culture, 74

Carmichael, Stokely, 99

Carnegie, Andrew, 4

Carter, Jimmy, 116, 118

Castro, Fidel, 65–66

Central Intelligence
    Agency (CIA), 65

Child labor, 11, 21, 43
Chinese Exclusion Act (1882), 9, 91
Christopher Street Liberation Day
    March, 102
Churchill, Winston, 55–56, 64
Civil Rights Act (1964), 90,
    97, 106–107
Civil Rights Act (1968), 100–101
Civil Rights Movement,
    77–81, 95–98
Civil War, 3
Civil War amendments, 5
Clinton, Bill, 134
Cold War, 48, 60–66, 129–131
Columbine High School
    massacre, 136
Committee on Public
    Information, 29
Communism, 58–60, 63–64,
    81–84, 91–94
Community Action Program, 90
Compromise of 1877, 5
Computers, 124–125, *124*
Congress of Racial Equality
    (CORE), 95
Congressional Reconstruction, 5
Conservative family values, 76
Consumer culture, 35
Coolidge, Calvin, 37
Corruption, 4
Counterculture movements,
    84–85, 105
Credit buying, 38–39
Cronkite, Walter, 109
Cuba, 12–13, 65–66

Cuban Missile Crisis, 65–66

D

Darwin, Charles, 11
D-Day, 46
De facto racism, 25
"Declaration of Negro Voters," 54
Demographic makeup, 8
Desegregation, 78–81, *80*
Diaspora, 25
Diem, Ngo Dinh, 91–93
Discrimination, 55, 71–72,
    98–99
Domestic terrorism, 134–136
Dot-com bubble, 126
Drug Enforcement Agency
    (DEA), 111
Du Bois, W. E. B., 11
Dust Bowl, 40

E

Economic Opportunity
    Act (1964), 90
Eisenhower, Dwight D., 46, 64–65,
    79, 83, 93
Equal Employment Opportunity
    Commission, 107
Equal Rights Amendment
    (ERA), 108
Escalation, 93–94
Espionage Act (1917), 29–30
European Union, 58
Executive Order 9981 (1948), 54
Expansionism, 12
Explorer I (satellite), 67

F

Fair Labor Standards Act
(1938), 21, 43
Falwell, Jerry, 116
Farmer, James, 95
Farnsworth, Clarence, 18
Faubus, Orval, 79
Federal Aid Highway Act
(1956), 70
Federal Assault Weapons
Ban, 134
Federal Bureau of Investigation
(FBI), 82, 135
Federal Deposit Insurance
Corporation (FDIC), 42
Federal Housing Authority
(FHA), 70
Feminine Mystique, The
(Friedan), 106
Final Solution, 44
Flappers, *35*
Floyd, George, 133
Ford, Gerald, 113, 115
Ford, Henry, 37
"Four Freedoms" speech
(Roosevelt), 54–55
Fourteen Points document
(Wilson), 31
France, 46
Freed, Alan, 77
Freedom Rides, 95–96
Freedom Summer, 98
Friedan, Betty, 106
Fuchs, Klaus, 82

G

Gay Activist Alliance, 102
Gay Liberation Front, 102
Gay Pride Day, 102
Germany, 27–28, 31, 44–46
GI Bill, 70
Gilded Age, 2–4, 9, 21
Goldwater, Barry, 115–116
Gompers, Samuel, 21
Gorbachev, Mikhail, 129–131
Great Depression, 39–44, 52
Great Migration, 24–25, 34
Great Society, 90–91, 116
Gun control, 133–136

H

Hammer v. Dagenhart, 21
Harding, Warren G., 37
Hayes, Rutherford B., 5
Head Start, 90
Hinckley, John, Jr., 133–134
Hine, Lewis, 11, 22
Hippies, 84–85
Hitler, Adolf, 44, 46
Hollywood Ten, 82
Hoover, Herbert, 37, 39–41
House Un-American Activities
Committee (HUAC), 81–82
How the Other Half Lives (Riis), 10
Human Be-In, 85
Hussein, Saddam, 128

I

Immigration, 7–9, 91

Immigration and Naturalization
	Act (1965), 91
Imperialism, 12–13, 27
Income tax, 118–119
Individualism, 39
Industrialization, 2–4, 9–10
Institutional racism, 53
International Ladies' Garment
	Workers' Union, 20
Internet, 125–127
Iran, 64–65, 117–118
Iran Hostage Crisis, 118, 128
Iraq, 128
Isolationism, 12–13, 37
Israel, 116–117, 128
Italy, 44

J

Japan, 45–48, 57
Jazz Age, 34
Jim Crow laws, 6, 24
Job Corps, 90
Johnson, Andrew, 5
Johnson, Lyndon B., 87, 89–91, 94,
	97–98, 100, 110, 112, 116
"Just Say No" campaign, 121

K

Kaczynski, Ted, 135
Keating-Owen Act (1916), 21
Kennedy, John F., 66, 87–89, 93,
	96–97, 112, 133
Kennedy, Robert F., 95–96
Kent State University, 110
Kerner Commission, 100

Khomeini, Ayatollah, 117–118
Khrushchev, Nikita, 66
Kim Il-Sung, 63
King, B. B., 77
King, Martin Luther, Jr., 81, 96–97,
	100, 133
King, Rodney, 131–132
Korean War, 63–64
Ku Klux Klan, 5, 98
Kuwait, 128

L

LA riots, 131–133, *132*
Labor movement, 20–22
Laissez-faire policies, 37
League of Nations, 31
Lend-Lease Act (1941), 45
Levitt, William, 72–74
LGBTQ rights movement, 101–102
Literacy tests, 98
Little Richard, 77
Little Rock Nine, 79
Lusitania (ship), 28

M

MacArthur, Douglas, 47, 57
Mao Zedong, 81
Marshall, George C., 58, 83
Marshall, Thurgood, 78
Marshall Plan, 58–60, *59*, 61
Martí, José, 12
Martin, Trayvon, 133
Mattachine Society, 102
McCarthy, Joseph, 82–84
McKinley, William, 12, 13, 14

McVeigh, Timothy, 134
Medicare and Medicaid Act (1965), 90
Mendez v. Westminster, 79
Meredith, James, 96
Mexican-American War, 12
Middle East, 116–118, 127–128
Midway, Battle of, 47
Militarism, 27
Military-industrial complex, 70
Minh, Ho Chi, 91–92
Montgomery bus boycott, 81, 95
Moral Majority, 116
Morgan, J. P., 4
Moses, Robert, 98
Mossadegh, Mohammad, 64–65, 117
Muckraking, 10–11
Muddy Waters, 77
Music, 77
Mussolini, Benito, 44, 46
Mutually assured destruction, 66

N

National Aeronautics and Space Administration (NASA), 67, 89
National American Woman Suffrage Association (NAWSA), 23
National Association for the Advancement of Colored People (NAACP), 54, 78
National Child Labor Committee (NCLC), 21

National Defense Education Act (NDEA), 67
National Organization for Women (NOW), 107
National Women's Party (NWP), 24
Nationalism, 27
Nativism, 8
Nazi Party, 44
Neutrality, 27–28, 45
New Deal, 33, 41–43, 52, 70
New Frontier, 88–89
New Jersey v. TLO, 137
New Right, 115–116
New York Factory Investigating Commission, 22
Newton, Huey P., 100
Nichols, Terry, 134
Nimitz, Chester W., 47
Nixon, Richard, 88, 110–115, *114*
North American Free Trade Agreement (NAFTA), 129
North Atlantic Treaty Organization (NATO), 62, 130

O

Oklahoma City bombing, 134, *135*
Operation Ajax, 64–65, 117
Operation Desert Storm, 128
Operation Iraqi Freedom, 128
Operation Rolling Thunder, 93
Organization of the Petroleum Exporting Countries (OPEC), 117, 127
Oswald, Lee Harvey, 89

P

Pacific Railway Act, 3–4
Paris Peace Conference, 31
Parks, Rosa, 80–81
Patrik, Linda, 135
Paul, Alice, 24
Peace Corps, 89
"Peace through Strength"
    strategy, 119
Pearl Harbor attack, 45
Persian Gulf War, 127–128
Philippines, 13
Plessy, Homer, 6
Plessy v. Ferguson, 6, 24
Potsdam Conference, 56–57
Presidential Reconstruction, 5
Presley, Elvis, 77
Progressive Era, 9–11, 14, 21–22
Prohibition, 36
Propaganda campaigns, 52
Proxy war, 64

R

Racism, 25, 53, 74. *See also*
    Discrimination; Segregation
Radio, 77
Randolph, A. Philip, 54
Reagan, Nancy, 121
Reagan, Ronald, 105, 116, 118–121,
    129, 131, 133–134
Reconstruction, 4–6, 24
Reconstruction Finance
    Corporation, 40
Red Scare, 81–84

Redlining, 73–74
Revenue Act (1964), 90
Ricci, Alessandra, 19–20
Riis, Jacob, 10–11
Robber barons, 4
Rockefeller, John D., 4
Rodwell, Craig, 102
Roe v. Wade, 109
Roosevelt, Eleanor, 42
Roosevelt, Franklin D., 33, 41, 45,
    47, 55–56, 70, 112
Roosevelt, Theodore, 14, 21,
    24, 26–27
Roosevelt Corollary, 27
Rosenberg, Julius and Ethel, 82
Russian Revolution (1917), 30

S

Sanger, Margaret, 11, 34
Saudi Arabia, 128
Schenck, Charles, 30
Schenck v. United States, 30
Schlafly, Phyllis, 108
School shootings, 136
Seale, Bobby, 100
Securities and Exchange
    Commission (SEC), 42
Sedition Act (1918), 30
Segregation, 6, 54–55, 74, 95. *See*
    also Desegregation
Selective Service Act
    (1917), 28–29
"Separate spheres" philosophy, 23
Servicemen's
    Readjustment Act, 70

Sharecroppers, 18, 24–25
Sinclair, Upton, 11
6888th Central Postal Directory
    Battalion, 54
Social change, 34–36
Social Darwinism, 11, 41
Social Security Act (1935), 43
Southern Christian Leadership
    Conference (SCLC), 81,
    95, 96, 98
Southern Manifesto, 80
Southern strategy, 111–113, 115
Soviet Union. *See* Union of Soviet
    Socialist Republics (USSR)
Space Race, 66–67
Spanish flu pandemic, 26
Spanish-American War, 12–13
Sputnik, 66–67
Stalin, Joseph, 56–57, 59, 61, 81
Statue of Liberty, 7
Steffens, Lincoln, 11
Stock market crash (1929), 39
Stonewall Rebellion, 101–102
Strategic Arms Reduction Treaty
    (START), 131
Strategic Defense Initiative
    (SDI), 119
Student Nonviolent Coordinating
    Committee (SNCC), 95, 98
Suburbs, 72–75, *73*
Summer of Love, 85
Supply and demand, 38

T

Taft, William Howard, 24

Tarbell, Ida, 11
Taylor, Breonna, 133
Technological advances,
    37, 124–127. *See*
    also Industrialization
Television, 76–77
Temperance movement, 36
Tenements, 8–9
Tet Offensive, 94, 109
Thatcher, Margaret, 130
Title IX, 107–108
Tito, Josip Broz, 60
Tonkin Gulf Resolution, 93
Trade Expansion Act (1962), 89
Treaty of Paris (1898), 13
Treaty of Versailles (1919), 31
Triangle Shirtwaist Factory, 22
Truman, Harry S., 47, 48, 54,
    56–57, 60, 61, 90
Truman Doctrine, 60, 61, 63–64
Tuskegee Airmen, 53

U

Unabomber, 135
Union of Soviet Socialist Republics
    (USSR), 56–64, 65–67,
    82, 129–131
United Nations, 56
Urbanization, 2, 10
USS *Maddox*, 93–94

V

Vanguard (satellite), 67
VENONA project, 82

Vietnam War, 65, 91–94,
    92, 109–111
Volunteers in Service to America
    (VISTA), 90

W

War on Drugs, 111, 112, 120–121
Warren, Earl, 84
Warren Commission, 89
Warsaw Pact, 63
Watergate scandal, 113–115
Wells, Ida B., 11
Wilson, Woodrow, 24, 28, 31
Women Airforce Service Pilots
    (WASPs), 52–53
Women's Army Auxiliary Corps
    (WAAC), 53, 54

Women's liberation movement,
    106–109, *107*
Women's suffrage
    movement, 22–24
World War I, 26–31
World War II, 45–48,
    52–55, 70, 78
World Wide Web, 126

Y

Yalta Conference, 56, 58, 61
Yom Kippur War, 128
Yugoslavia, 60, 130

Z

Zapruder film, 89
Zimmermann Telegram, 28

ACKNOWLEDGMENTS

I'd like to thank my family first, for putting up with me being a little stressed while writing this book: my husband, Bill; daughter, Willa; dog, Sasha; mom, Mary; dad, Charlie; and brother, Michael. Other people I'd like to thank for always being supportive of my endeavors in general are friends Shannon Sutlief, Courtney Caldwell, Christine Connolly, Brandy Glover, Nancy Larsen, Karen Barton, Kendra Burt, Heather Kidd, Linda Havins, and Jeff Sullivan.

Additionally, I had never written a book before, and my editor, Barbara Isenberg, was extremely patient with me and so helpful! Finally, though I haven't seen him in 20 or more years, that American history professor who made me love history was Dr. John Daly (no, not the golfer!). He taught me at Austin College in Sherman, Texas, in the mid-1990s but is now teaching at the State University of New York. (Thanks, internet!)

ABOUT THE AUTHOR

 **Carrie Cagle** lives in a suburb of Dallas, Texas, with her husband, daughter, and grumpy dachshund. When not writing history books, she loves to sew, bake, and binge-watch historical dramas. She has been a high school teacher for 20 years and has taught AP US history, AP government, AP European history, AP psychology, American history, and world history. Carrie has BAs in psychology and history and an MS in curriculum and instruction. Her social studies curriculum can be found online at bit.ly/i-heart-history.

CPSIA information can be obtained
at www.ICGtesting.com
Printed in the USA
JSHW051252180722
28018JS00002B/3